The Epic Geography Quiz Book

Mac Trivia

Table of Contents

World Geography - Quiz 1

Answers on page 207

1. Which continent is home to the most independent countries?

2. 1600 Pennsylvania Avenue is home to which famous residence?

3. Constanta is a city on the shores of the Black Sea in the south east of which country?

4. Which sea separates Europe from Africa?

5. Lake Toba is a large natural lake occupying the caldera of the Toba supervolcano. In which country would you find it?

6. What is the brightest city on Earth from space?

   a. Las Vegas
   b. Tokyo
   c. New York City
   d. Hong Kong

7. The cities of Erbil and Basra can be found in which country?

8. What is the only country that passes through both the Equator and the Tropic of Capricorn?

9. What is the second-highest mountain in the world?

10. In which country is the Sinai Peninsula located?

a. Israel
b. Egypt
c. Jordan
d. Turkey

11. One of the deepest estuaries in the world, the Gulf of St Lawrence is located off the coast of which country?

12. What is the official currency of Saudi Arabia?

13. What is the largest desert in the world?

14. Easter Island is a territory of which South
    American country?

    a. Chile
    b. Peru
    c. Argentina
    d. Colombia

15. Albuquerque is the largest city in which US
    state?

16. How many time zones are there in China?

17. The Giza Plateau can be found in which
    country?

18. What name is given to a major wind system
    that seasonally reverses its direction?

    a. Hurricane
    b. Typhoon
    c. Monsoon
    d. Tornado

19. Quito is the capital city of which South
    American country?

20. Okinawa is surrounded by the East China Sea and Pacific Ocean. To which country does it belong?

Africa Geography - Quiz 1

Answers on page 208

1. Mogadishu is the capital city of which African country?

   a. Nigeria
   b. Kenya
   c. Somalia
   d. Uganda

2. What colour background does the national flag of Tunisia have?

3. Which former French colony was, until the late 1950s, one of the largest wine producing countries in the world?

4. The *Cradle of Humankind* is a paleoanthropological site located in which country?

   a. Ghana
   b. Namibia
   c. Angola
   d. South Africa

5. Victoria Falls is located on the border of Zambia and which other country?

6. Which ocean is Comoros located in?

7. What is the largest lake in Africa?

8. Which country is home to the Skeleton Coast, the world's largest ship graveyard?

9. Mombasa is a coastal city in which country?

10. Which mountain range runs through Morocco, Algeria and Tunisia?

11. Off the coast of Mozambique lies the island of Madagascar. What is the name of the body of water separating the two?

12. Libreville is the capital city of which country?

    a. Gabon
    b. Ghana
    c. The Gambia
    d. Equatorial Guinea

13. With which country does Mozambique share its longest land border of nearly 1000 miles?

    a. Malawi
    b. Zambia
    c. Zimbabwe
    d. South Africa

14. The island of Zanzibar is part of which country?

15. In which city would you find South Africa's National Gallery?

16. What is the body of water to the north that the River Nile flows into?

17. Lake Assal is a crater lake in the Danakil Desert but which country is it in?

    a. Tanzania
    b. Djibouti
    c. Cameroon
    d. Nigeria

18. What is the capital city of Ghana?

19. What is the official language of Nigeria?

20. The Libyan Desert is part of which larger desert
    system?

Asia Geography - Quiz 1

Answers on page 208

1. What is China's longest river?

2. Which central Asian country is home to a crater
   nicknamed *The Door to Hell*?

   a. Tajikistan
   b. Turkmenistan
   c. Iran
   d. Afghanistan

3. Which country's flag features a cedar tree?

4. Which two countries is Bhutan sandwiched
   between?

5. Which sea is located between mainland China
   and the Korean Peninsula?

6. On which island of Japan is the city of Sapporo
   located?

7. Borobudur Temple is the largest Buddhist
   temple in the world. Which country is it in?

8. Hemis, Gangotri, and Namdapha are all national parks in which country?

    a. India
    b. Pakistan
    c. Nepal
    d. Sri Lanka

9. Which river in Southeast Asia passes through China, Cambodia, Myanmar, Laos, Thailand, and Vietnam?

10. The Gulf of Tonkin is a crescent-shaped body of water situated off South China and the northern part of which other country?

11. Which Southeast Asian country is made up of over 17,000 islands and is the largest archipelago in the world?

12. The ancient city of Samarkand is in what modern-day country?

13. What is the largest city in Pakistan?

14. Which country has the lowest population density in Asia?

    a. Turkmenistan

    b. Mongolia

    c. Bhutan

    d. Oman

15. The cities of Ipoh and Kuala Lumpur can be found in which country?

16. Beppu is a city famous for its hot springs. Which country is it in?

    a. South Korea

    b. Japan

    c. Taiwan

    d. Vietnam

17. What is the capital city of Laos?

    a. Vientiane

    b. Phnom Penh

    c. Phuket

    d. Nha Trang

18. What is the largest desert in Asia?

19. Jeddah is a Saudi Arabian port city on the coast
     of which sea?

20. In which Chinese city can you find the imperial
     palace complex Forbidden City?

Capital Cities - Quiz 1

Answers on page 209

1. What is the capital city of the United Arab Emirates?

2. Podgorica is the capital of which European country?

3. What is the capital city of Colombia?

4. What is the capital city of Jordan?

5. Which capital city sits on the River Vistula?

    a. Warsaw
    b. Belgrade
    c. Tallinn
    d. Riga

6. Which capital city sits 3,640 metres above sea level, making it the highest in the world?

7. What is the southernmost capital city in Europe?

8. Which capital city sits on the Absheron
    Peninsula on the Caspian Sea?

9. Tegucigalpa is the capital city of which
    mountainous country in Central America?

    a. El Salvador
    b. Nicaragua
    c. Haiti
    d. Honduras

10. In which capital city would you be if you had
     visited Grafton Street and the Ha'penny bridge?

11. Which capital city is home to attractions such as
     the East Side Gallery and Checkpoint Charlie?

12. Tashkent is the capital city of which country?

13. What is the capital city of Indonesia?

14. What is the capital city of Liberia?

     a. Greenville
     b. Monrovia
     c. Abidjan

d. Freetown

15. Addis Ababa is the capital of which African country?

16. What is the capital city of Paraguay?

    a. Asunción
    b. San Lorenzo
    c. Montevideo
    d. Sucre

17. Asmara is the capital city of which East African country?

    a. Djibouti
    b. Eritrea
    c. Sudan
    d. Somalia

18. What is the capital city of Cambodia?

19. What is the capital city of Spain?

20. What is the capital city of Turkey?

Europe Geography - Quiz 1

Answers on page 210

1. Dalmatia is an area of which European country?

2. The Elbphilharmonie is a concert hall in which German city?

3. What city in northern Spain is home to Frank Gehry's Guggenheim Museum?

4. The Azores are an autonomous region of which country?

5. The Palme d'Or is the most prestigious prize at the annual film festival in which French town?

6. What is mainland Europe's northernmost capital city?

    a. Stockholm
    b. Helsinki
    c. Oslo
    d. Tallinn

7. The Mediterranean island of Corsica belongs to which European country?

8. Which island nation is the most sparsely populated country in Europe?

9. Which of these is an airport in a Turkish city of the same name?

   a. Superman
   b. Batman
   c. Antman
   d. Spiderman

10. If you were buying flowers at the Columbia Road Flower market, which city would you be in?

11. The Danish capital, Copenhagen, boasts a statue of what famous character from the stories of Hans Christian Andersen?

12. In which Italian port city was Christopher Columbus born?

13. Lake Annecy is located in which country?

14. Which Spanish Island is known as *The Island of Eternal Spring*?

15. Naxos is the largest of which Greek island group?

    a. The Cyclades
    b. The Ioanians
    c. The Dodecanese
    d. The Saronic

16. Lake Ohrid straddles the border between North Macedonia and which other country?

17. What is the most densely populated country in Europe?

    a. Malta
    b. Monaco
    c. San Marino
    d. Vatican City

18. Varna is a port city and seaside resort in which European country?

19. If you were taking the train from Graz to Maribor, you'd be travelling from Austria to

which country?

20. Which region of Spain is the Sierra Nevada
    mountain range located?

    a. Andalucia
    b. Murcia
    c. Galicia
    d. Aragon

Geology - Quiz 1

Answers on page 211

1. After which type of natural disaster would pyroclastic flow most likely occur?

2. What type of rock is granite?

3. In which country can the Sierra Morena mountain range be found?

   a. Portugal
   b. Spain
   c. Italy
   d. Andorra

4. In which country is the Mayon Volcano located?

5. The Mesoamerican Reef is the largest barrier reef in the Western Hemisphere. How long does it stretch?

   a. 225 miles
   b. 425 miles
   c. 625 miles
   d. 825 miles

6. What does the Richter scale measure?

7. In which country is Mount Merapi located?

8. Located in India, what is the Rann of Kutch?

    a. Mountain
    b. Salt Marsh
    c. Lake
    d. Canyon

9. Which mountain range passes through Banff National Park?

10. In which country would you find the Great Dividing Range?

11. The Vinson Massif is the highest mountain of which continent?

12. What name is given to the long, narrow inlets on Norway's coast formed by glaciers during the last ice age?

13. What type of geological feature is Popocatepetl in Mexico?

a. Canyon

b. Cave

c. Geyser

d. Volcano

14. Formed by the Forth Glacier during the last ice age, which estuary in Scotland separates West Lothian from Fife?

15. In which country is Mount Asahi located?

16. The Giant's Causeway, known for its unique basalt columns, is located in which country of the UK?

17. One of the largest cave systems in Europe, the Frasassi Caves are located in which country?

18. Steamboat Geyser is the world's tallest active geyser. Which country is it located in?

19. Jeju Island is a volcanic island, dominated at its centre by Mount Hallasan, an extinct volcano 1,950 metres high and the highest mountain in which Asian country?

20. What is the name given to the ancient remains
     of living things preserved in rocks?

Guess the Country - Quiz 1

Answers on page 212

1. Zermatt is a popular ski resort in which country?

2. Which country was painter Frida Kahlo from?

3. Established in 1290, in which country would you find the University of Coimbra?

4. Which country's flag features a Union Jack and exactly 6 stars?

5. By population, Auckland is the largest city in which country?

6. In which country is the tallest building in Europe?

   a. United Kingdom
   b. Poland
   c. Russia
   d. Spain

7. Which African country is home to the *Avenue of the Baobabs*?

a. Madagascar

b. Burundi

c. Lesotho

d. Chad

8. Which country's flag features a trident?

9. Which country in East Africa is renowned for its wildlife and home to Masai Mara National Reserve and Nairobi National Park?

10. In which country is The Day of the Dead Festival traditionally celebrated every year on 1st and 2nd November?

11. What is the largest country in Southeast Asia?

12. The ancient city of Petra is located in which country?

13. What is the third-largest island in the Caribbean?

14. Pho and Banh Mi are dishes from which country?

15. Which country's flag features an AK-47 rifle?

    a. Chad
    b. Senegal
    c. Algeria
    d. Mozambique

16. In which country can you walk the Camino de Santiago?

17. Baldwin Street is officially the steepest street in the world with an angle of 38 degrees. Which country is it in?

18. Which country is nicknamed *Land of the Midnight Sun*?

19. Which country is home to the world's largest airport, which covers 300 square miles?

    a. China
    b. Saudi Arabia
    c. Russia
    d. USA

20. Which landlocked country between Russia and China has a giant statue depicting its country's

founder on horseback?

Landmarks - Quiz 1

Answers on page 213

1. Which tower was built between 1887 and 1889 to commemorate 100 years since the end of the French Revolution?

2. Architecturally the longest and widest staircase in Europe, which steps link together Piazza di Spagna and Piazza Trinità dei Monti?

3. On its completion in January 1943, which US government building was the world's largest office building?

4. East Side Gallery is a memorial and a remnant of which wall?

5. Which famous presidential monument was sculpted by Gutzon Borglum?

6. In which city is Juliet's Balcony located?

7. Which New York City skyscraper hosts an annual race, where competitors race from the ground level up to the 86th floor observation

deck?

8. In which city is the colourful, fairytale-like Saint Basil's Cathedral located?

9. Which Dubai hotel famously has 7 stars?

10. Which statue of a young boy has become the symbol of Brussels?

11. Best known as the inspiration behind Disneyland's Sleeping Beauty Castle, which castle in Germany was built solely for King Ludwig II?

12. Which statue sits on top of Corcovado Mountain, which means "hunchback" in Portuguese, overlooking Rio de Janeiro?

13. Marienplatz is the central square in which German city?

14. The Golden Temple in Amritsar is one of the holiest sites in Sikhism. In which region of India is it located?

15. Which British castle was built atop Castle Rock, an extinct volcano?

16. After almost 2000 years since its construction, which building in Italy still holds the record for the largest unreinforced concrete dome in the world?

17. The Liberty Bell, an iconic symbol of American independence, is located in which city?

18. The Arashiyama Bamboo Forest is a tourist attraction in which Japanese city?

19. Designed by the same company, which UK bridge is said to have inspired the Sydney Harbour Bridge?

20. In which country are the Batu Caves located?

North America Geography - Quiz 1

Answers on page 214

1. Mount Aripo is the highest mountain on which Caribbean island?

2. Spokane is a city in which US state?

3. Which American state is nicknamed *Cornhusker State*?

4. Which US state is located directly north of Iowa?

    a. Minnesota
    b. South Dakota
    c. Indiana
    d. Maryland

5. Nassau is the capital of which Caribbean island?

6. Tortuguero National Park in Costa Rica is named after which animal, its most famous annual visitors?

    a. Tapirs
    b. Tarantulas

c. Turtles

d. Toucans

7. What is Canada's most populated city?

8. In which US city can you visit Fisherman's Wharf neighbourhood on the waterfront?

9. The Gatun Locks, Pedro Miguel Locks, and Miraflores Locks are locks in which major canal?

10. Which dam on the Colorado River was formerly known as the Boulder Dam?

11. Which of these US states does NOT have a Pacific coastline?

a. Arizona

b. California

c. Washington

d. Oregon

12. What state of Mexico is the ancient Mayan city of Uxmal located in?

a. Hidalgo

b. Sinaloa

c. Tabasco

d. Yucatan

13. What is the capital city of Jamaica?

14. By area, what is the smallest US state?

15. What colour features on the flag of Honduras,
     Guatemala, Belize, and Cuba?

16. Stanley Park is an urban park in which Canadian
     city?

17. The Four Corners Monument marks the
     quadripoint in the Southwestern United States
     where the states of Arizona, Colorado, New
     Mexico and which other state meet?

18. Which US city is known as *The Windy City*?

19. Which Caribbean country is famous for its
     Pitons, a pair of volcanic spires that are
     UNESCO World Heritage Sites?

20. El Salvador and which other country border
     Guatemala to the south?

Oceania Geography - Quiz 1

Answers on page 214

1. Todd River is located in which country?

2. In which ocean is Fiji located?

3. The Great Barrier Reef is off the coast of which Australian state?

4. True or false: Dunedin is a city in New Zealand?

5. What is the name of the strait that divides New Zealand's north and south islands?

6. What is the largest lake in New Zealand?

   a. Lake Taupō
   b. Lake Whakatipu
   c. Lake Wanaka
   d. Lake Matheson

7. The Bikini Atoll is a world famous dive site having been used as a ship graveyard in WW2. Which country is it in?

   a. Fiji

b. Samoa

c. Marshall Islands

d. Tuvalu

8. What is the capital of Australia's island-state Tasmania?

9. Guam, an unincorporated territory of the USA, is the largest island in Micronesia but is it closer to Hawaii or Japan?

10. Which city is home to New Zealand's tallest building?

11. Australia's Shark Bay is home to the world's largest population of which of these marine mammals?

a. Humpback Whales

b. Dugongs

c. Porpoises

d. Bottlenose Dolphins

12. In which country is the Tanami Desert?

13. In which territory or state is Australia's capital city, Canberra, located?

14. Which 150 mile Australian road was built by soldiers who had returned from WW1?

    a. The Big Lap
    b. The Great Ocean Road
    c. Gibb River Road
    d. The Great Barrier Reef Drive

15. Hawke's Bay is a region in New Zealand known for its wineries. Is it located on the North or South Island?

16. What is the name of the indigenous people of New Zealand?

17. Bondi Beach is a famous beach in which Australian city?

18. What is the Pacific Ocean's smallest country?

    a. Kiribati
    b. Nauru
    c. Palau

d. Tonga

19. Geelong is a port city located in what country?

20. Which animal outnumbers humans in New Zealand by around five to one?

Rivers, Seas & Oceans - Quiz 1

Answers on page 215

1. The island of Tahiti is in which ocean?

2. What body of water separates Italy and Croatia?

3. The Aare river runs through the capital city of which country?

4. Which is both the world's oldest and deepest lake?

   a. Lake Baikal
   b. Lake Superior
   c. Lake Huron
   d. Great Bear Lake

5. Into which sea does the River Nile flow?

6. At 1100 miles, the longest man-made canal in the world is found in which country?

7. River Korana flows through Bosnia and Herzegovina, and which other country?

8. What is the largest island in the Indian Ocean?

9. Which river flows through Florence?

10. Which sea is found between Greece and
Turkey?

a. Aegean Sea
b. Mediterranean Sea
c. Black Sea
d. Red Sea

11. What is the longest river in Ireland?

12. In which ocean is the Seychelles located?

13. The River Danube crosses through how many
countries?

a. 4
b. 6
c. 8
d. 10

14. Tampa Bay is a large open-water estuary and
part of which gulf?

15. Where would you find the Sea of Tranquility?

16. By area, Lake Volta is the world's largest dam reservoir. In which country is it located?

    a. Brazil
    b. Russia
    c. Spain
    d. Ghana`

17. Which sea does the River Thames flow into?

18. Which waterfall is southwest of Colombia's capital city, Bogota?

    a. Victoria Falls
    b. Tequendama Falls
    c. Angel Falls
    d. Tugela Falls

19. Which UK city sits on the River Clyde?

20. Which ocean borders British Columbia in Canada?

South America Geography - Quiz 1

Answers on page 216

1. The Maipo Valley is a wine region in which country?

2. What part of South America is sometimes referred to as *land of the big feet?*

3. Which country is the only country in South America to have English as its official language?

4. What is the largest lake in South America?

5. Which famous statue overlooks the city of Rio de Janeiro from the top of Corcovado Mountain?

6. Costa Rica shares a land border with Nicaragua and which other country?

7. In which country would you find the capital city Paramaribo?

   a. Guatemala
   b. Uruguay
   c. Venezuela

d. Suriname

8. Paraguay has borders with Argentina, Brazil and which other country?

9. What is the traditional music genre associated with Argentina, known for its dramatic and passionate movements?

10. In which country would you be if you were visiting Kaieteur Falls - the world's tallest single drop waterfall?

   a. Peru
   b. Ecuador
   c. Guyana
   d. Venezuela

11. Where is the Kourou space centre located?

   a. French Guiana
   b. Suriname
   c. El Salvador
   d. Belize

12. The Nazca Lines are a UNESCO World Heritage Site in which country?

13. The Galapagos Islands are part of which country?

14. What was discovered in Venezuela's Lake Maracaibo in 1914?

    a. Oil
    b. Gold
    c. Diamonds
    d. Pearls

15. On one of the many long stretches of road that comprise the Pan-American Highway, there is a very large missing link about 54 miles long, where no road exists. It's known as the Darien Gap. It falls into two countries - on one side is Panama; which country is on the other?

    a. Colombia
    b. Venezuela
    c. Bolivia
    d. Nicaragua

16. In which country can you undertake the W Trek?

17. Iguazu Falls lie on the border between
     Argentina and which other country?

18. What is the southernmost city in the world,
     located in Argentina?

19. What colour is the rhombus on Brazil's flag?

20. AEP is the IATA code for which major city's
     airport?

Sports Geography - Quiz 1

Answers on page 217

1. In which city would you find Portman Road stadium?

2. Which country is home to the world's largest football stadium with a capacity of 114,000?

    a. Mexico
    b. USA
    c. Germany
    d. North Korea

3. In which city is tennis played at Roland Garros?

4. In which city was the 1992 Summer Olympic Games held?

5. Which men's national football team is sometimes referred to as the Oranje?

6. The Ryōgoku Kokugikan arena in Tokyo is the main venue for which Japanese sport?

7. What sport do the Toronto Maple Leafs play?

8. The 1994 Winter Olympics was held in Lillehammer. Which country is Lillehammer in?

9. If you were at a game at Eden Park in Auckland, what sport would you be watching?

10. Spain won the 2010 FIFA World Cup. Which country was the tournament held in?

11. What sport is played at The Rose Bowl in Southampton?

12. *The Powerpuff Girls*, or *Las Chicas Superpoderosas*, is the nickname for the women's football team of which South American country?

13. In which city would you find Elland Road Stadium?

14. The MCG is a cricket stadium situated in Yarra Park in which Australian city?

15. The New York Red Bulls play which sport?

16. The Orioles and the Ravens are sports teams
    from which US city?

17. Which team plays their home games at the
    Santiago Bernabeu?

18. In which country was the 2023 Rugby Union
    World Cup held?

    a. Japan
    b. France
    c. Australia
    d. South Africa

19. What is the northernmost racetrack to have
    held a Formula One race?

    a. Silverstone
    b. Zandvoort
    c. Monza
    d. Montreal

20. Where were the 1964 Summer Olympics held?

    a. Moscow
    b. London
    c. Tokyo

d. Los Angeles

United Kingdom Geography - Quiz 1

Answers on page 218

1. What is the smallest county in the UK?

2. Which county is Stonehenge situated in?

    a. Somerset
    b. Wiltshire
    c. Monmouthshire
    d. Devon

3. In which century did the Leeds and Liverpool Canal first open for use?

4. Which two 'London' airports are located in Essex?

5. Which of these rivers forms a natural border between Devon and Cornwall?

    a. Severn
    b. Avon
    c. Tamar
    d. Wye

6. In which county would you find the seaside town of Cromer?

7. Which landmark, designed by Antony Gormley, stands on the former pit head baths, next to the A1?

8. The Menai Suspension bridge spans the Menai Strait, connecting mainland Wales to which island?

9. The towns of Hinckley, Market Harborough, and Coalville are located in which English county?

10. Which Derbyshire town is home to the parish church St Mary and All Saints, famous for its crooked spire?

11. To what group of islands does the island of Barra belong?

12. The M20 motorway runs through what English county?

13. At 310 metres at its deepest point, what is the deepest loch in Scotland?

a. Loch Morar

b. Loch Lomond

c. Loch Lochy

d. Loch Ness

14. In which coastal city would you find the i360 observation tower?

15. Jaguar Land Rover has its headquarters in which UK city?

16. Which city is home to attractions including the Jane Austen Centre, Pulteney Bridge, and the Royal Crescent?

17. In which county is Wentworth Golf Club located?

a. Essex

b. Surrey

c. Hertfordshire

d. Warwickshire

18. What is the only city in Cumbria?

19. The longest train route in the UK is 722 miles,
     starting in Aberdeen and finishing where?

20. Durdle Door is a natural limestone arch on
     which famous coastline?

World Geography - Quiz 2

Answers on page 219

1. What is the capital of the Canadian province of Alberta?

2. The US military installation Area 51 is located in which state?

3. The Gulf of Guinea lies on the west coast of which continent?

4. In which country can you drive along the Wild Atlantic Way, the longest uninterrupted coastal route in the world at 1600 miles?

   a. Ireland
   b. Canada
   c. Iceland
   d. Argentina

5. In which country is the Lut desert?

   a. Iraq
   b. Egypt
   c. Iran

d. China

6. Which coastal African country is bordered by
   Algeria and Libya?

7. What bird is on Mexico's flag?

8. How many time zones does mainland USA
   have?

9. The Mariana Trench is the deepest ocean trench,
   deeper than Mount Everest is tall, but which
   ocean is it in?

10. The Danyang-Kunshan Grand Bridge is the
    world's longest bridge with a total length of
    103 miles. Which country is it in?

11. The Daintree Rainforest is considered to be the
    world's oldest rainforest. Where is it located?

12. The Cape of Good Hope is a rocky headland on
    the southern tip of which continent?

13. In which country would you find the pilgrimage
    cities of Mecca and Medina?

14. What is the capital city of Nigeria?

15. In which city is the world's tallest building, the
     Burj Khalifa, located?

16. Which country has the highest percentage of its
     land mass covered in forest?

     a. Finland
     b. Norway
     c. Suriname
     d. Canada

17. What is the largest city, based on population, in
     the Southern Hemisphere?

18. Mount Vinson is the highest mountain where?

     a. The Arctic
     b. The Antarctic
     c. The Himalayas
     d. South America

19. Malé is the capital city of which archipelago
     nation?

20. Which country in Oceania is known as *The Land of the Long White Cloud?*

Africa Geography - Quiz 2

Answers on page 220

1. Dakar is the capital city of which West African country?

    a. The Gambia
    b. Mauritania
    c. Senegal
    d. Guinea

2. The longest bridge in Africa, the 12.7 mile 6th October Bridge, is situated in which country?

    a. Egypt
    b. Nigeria
    c. Kenya
    d. South Africa

3. Botswana is home to which desert?

4. In which country would you find the Garden Route?

5. Lilongwe is the capital of which country?

a. Rwanda

b. Malawi

c. Zambia

d. Mozambique

6. In which country is the famous monolith The
   Zuma Rock located?

7. What is the official language of Sao Tome
   and Principe?

8. Mount Kilimanjaro, the highest peak in
   Africa, is located in which country?

9. Which African capital city is known as *The
   White*, for its whitewashed buildings?

10. Which country's flag features a machete?

    a. Algeria

    b. Angola

    c. Burundi

    d. Chad

11. Which ocean does the Limpopo River drain
    into?

12. The largest city in the world without a major river is located in Africa. Which city is it?

13. What is the official language of Togo?

14. The Pyramids of Giza, one of the Seven Wonders of the Ancient World, are located in which country?

15. Madagascar is the fourth largest island in the world, but its economy is heavily reliant on agriculture. What crop is the country the world's largest producer of?

16. What is the name of the large grasslands in Tanzania where wildlife thrives?

17. What is Nigeria's largest city?

18. Which country is NOT located in West Africa?

    a. Liberia
    b. Togo
    c. Burundi
    d. Senegal

19. Africa's biggest dam is located on the Blue
    Nile River, but in which country is it situated?

    a. Ethiopia
    b. South Sudan
    c. Sudan
    d. Egypt

20. If you visited the *Wadi al-Hitan*, or *Whale
    Valley*, in which country would you be?

    a. Egypt
    b. Tanzania
    c. Niger
    d. Libya

Asia Geography - Quiz 2

Answers on page 220

1. In which country would you find the Yellow River?

2. Qatar is a peninsular Arab country in which gulf?

3. The King Fahd Causeway connects Bahrain with which country?

4. Spanning 500 acres, Angkor Wat is a Hindu-Buddhist temple complex in which country?

5. Islamabad and Hyderabad are cities in which country?

6. In which city are the Petronas Towers located?

7. Nong Khai is a border town popular with tourists on which country's border with Laos?

8. Gardens by the Bay is a waterfront nature
    park in which Asian city?

    a. Hong Kong
    b. Singapore
    c. Tokyo
    d. Taipei

9. The Monastery, the Treasury, and the Palace
    Tomb are the popular names of sites in
    which ancient Middle Eastern city?

    a. Babylon
    b. Damascus
    c. Petra
    d. Baalbek

10. The summit of Mount Everest is on the
    border of China and which other country?

11. The Malabar Coast is situated on which
    country's south western coastline?

12. Davao, Cebu, and Bacolod are cities in which
    Asian country?

    a. Vietnam

b. Laos

c. Philippines

d. Malaysia

13. The Tibetan Plateau, known as the *Roof of the World*, is mostly located in which country?

14. Brunei is a tiny nation situated on which island?

15. Which animal features on the flag of Sri Lanka?

16. India's Valley of Flowers National Park is a UNESCO World Heritage Site, featuring stunning exotic flowers against backdrops of the Himalayas. Which region is it located in?

    a. Darjeeling
    b. Uttarakhand
    c. Bihar
    d. Odisha

17. What is the second largest city in Japan by population?

18. The Taipei 101 is the tallest building in which country?

19. Which sea lies to the north of Turkey?

20. If you were landing at Incheon International Airport, which country would you be in?

Capital Cities - Quiz 2

Answers on page 221

1. What is the capital city of Oman?

2. What is the capital city of Sri Lanka?

3. What is the capital city of Mongolia?

    a. Astana
    b. Samarkand
    c. Ulaanbaatar
    d. Tashkent

4. What is the capital city of Australia?

5. The city of Ouagadougou is the capital of which West African country?

    a. Burkina Faso
    b. Senegal
    c. Cameroon
    d. Ivory Coast

6. What is the capital city of the Netherlands?

7. Victoria is the capital city of which Indian Ocean archipelago nation?

8. What is the capital city of Croatia?

9. Which country's capital city translates as 'good airs' or 'fair winds'?

10. What is the capital city of Russia?

11. What is the capital city of North Macedonia?

12. Which European capital city is home to the 25th April Bridge, the longest suspension bridge in Europe?

13. What is the capital city of Barbados?

14. What is the capital city of Iraq?

   a. Basra
   b. Erbil
   c. Baghdad
   d. Mosul

15. What is the capital city of Bahrain?

a. Manama

b. Tehran

c. Sana'a

d. Muscat

16. What is the capital city of North Korea?

17. What is the capital city of Samoa?

a. Apia

b. Funafuti

c. Suva

d. Nusantara

18. What is the capital city of India?

19. Which capital city is home to the Olympic
stadium nicknamed The Bird's Nest?

20. Which capital city is home to the
headquarters of Spotify?

Europe Geography - Quiz 2

Answers on page 222

1. In which city would you find the Spanish Steps?

2. Sofia is the capital of which country?

3. If you were flying into El Prat airport, which city would you be landing in?

4. Oulu and Rovaniemi are cities in which European country?

5. Lusitania was the Roman name for which country?

6. Which country has a record 45 UNESCO World Heritage sites?

7. The Tivoli Gardens, one of the oldest amusement parks in the world, is located in which city?

8. The GR20 is a footpath across which Mediterranean island?

a. Malta

b. Sardinia

c. Corfu

d. Corsica

9. Shaftesbury Avenue in London runs north-east from what famous crossroads?

10. In which city would you find the International Court of Justice?

11. Situated in a glacially formed basin, Lake Bohinj is a paradise for swimming, hiking and biking. Which country is it in?

12. In which country is the city Brno?

13. The River Aire flows through which UK city?

14. Which city in Italy is dubbed the *Florence of the South*?

15. In which city would you find Schönbrunn Palace?

16. In which city would you find the 16th century fortification Belém Tower?

17. Which country is home to Bran Castle, the castle which inspired Count Dracula?

18. Which large forest, located in central Germany, is known for its dense woodlands and fairy-tale legends?

19. Bansko is a ski resort situated in which European country?

20. Which European city is home to the world's largest museum?

Geology - Quiz 2

Answers on page 223

1. Part of the East Africa Rift, the Erta Ale is which country's most active volcano and one of just six active lava lakes on Earth?

   a. Djibouti
   b. Eritrea
   c. Ethiopia
   d. Somalia

2. Covering an area four times larger and deeper than the legendary Grand Canyon, the Copper Canyon is a series of six massive canyons in which Mexican state?

   a. Chihuahua
   b. Yucatan
   c. Durango
   d. Puebla

3. Which country has the largest number of active volcanoes?

   a. Iceland
   b. Italy

c. Ethiopia

d. Indonesia

4. What is the local nickname for the Mexican volcano Popocatépeti?

a. Popeye
b. El Popo
c. Papa
d. Padre

5. What name is given to molten rocks thrown out by a volcano?

6. What is the name of Ethiopia's highly volcanic region, famed for its multicoloured hot springs?

a. Dallol
b. Akutan
c. Cotopaxi
d. Katmai

7. Uluru, Australia's most iconic landmark, is formed of what type of rock?

a. Limestone

b. Sandstone

c. Shale

d. Granite

8. What type of rock is formed by heat and pressure acting on existing rocks?

9. What is the name of the supercontinent that existed around 300 million years ago?

10. Which layer of Earth lies directly beneath the crust?

11. Which tectonic plate is the largest?

a. The Pacific Plate

b. The North American Plate

c. The Eurasian Plate

d. The African Plate

12. What is the name for a large mass of ice that moves slowly over land?

13. What is the hardest natural mineral on Earth?

14. What is the name of the process by which
    water, ice, or wind removes soil and rock?

15. What geological feature is created when
    two continental plates collide?

16. What is the main component of the Earth's
    core?

    a. Titanium
    b. Lead
    c. Iron
    d. Zinc

17. Sapphire is usually which colour?

18. What is the name of the volcano that
    erupted in 1883, causing one of the loudest
    sounds in recorded history?

19. Which rock forms the greater part of the
    White Cliffs of Dover?

20. Stalactites and stalagmites are limestone
    foundations found where?

Guess The Country - Quiz 2

Answers on page 224

1. Stellenbosch and Paarl are popular
   wine-making towns in which country?

2. Which Caribbean country is famous for its
   rum, cigars, and colonial architecture,
   particularly in its capital, Havana?

3. Which country is nicknamed *India's
   Teardrop?*

4. Which country is home to cities including
   Coimbra, Evora, and Braga?

5. Adobo is widely considered the national dish
   of which country?

6. What is the third-largest island in the
   Mediterranean?

7. Which country is home to Gouda, famous for
   its cheese?

8. In which country would you find the UNESCO World Heritage Site of Shibam Hadramawt? The town is famed for having the world's highest mud-brick buildings, from which it gets the nickname *The Manhattan of the Desert*?

    a. Oman
    b. Jordan
    c. Lebanon
    d. Yemen

9. In which country was the world's first purpose-built racetrack opened in 1907?

10. The huge waterfall Skógafoss is located on which island country?

11. Which European country has the *lev* as its currency?

12. The flag of which country features a yellow cross on a blue background?

13. Which country would you be in if you were served *dolmades* and *taramosalata*?

14. A *jeepney* is a type of bus popular in which Southeast Asian country?

15. Which country has its own film industry called Nollywood?

16. Malbork Castle is the largest castle in the world by area. Which country is it in?

    a. Germany
    b. Poland
    c. Slovakia
    d. Romania

17. Which country produces drinks such as Vinho Verde and Ginja?

18. What is the southernmost Caribbean country?

    a. Barbados
    b. Trinidad and Tobago
    c. Cuba
    d. St Kitts and Nevis

19. Which country has the most official languages?

a. South Africa

b. Bolivia

c. India

d. Zimbabwe

20. Paul David Hewson aka Bono is from which country?

Landmarks - Quiz 2

Answers on page 225

1. Which palace in Granada in Spain is known as the Red Castle or the Red Fortress?

2. What is the tallest building in the UK?

3. The Hollywood Walk of Fame, which consists of 2,800 five-pointed terrazzo-and-brass stars embedded into the pavement, is located on which street in Los Angeles?

4. Who designed Casa Batlló, one of Europe's strangest residential buildings?

5. In which country can you swim in the geothermal Blue Lagoon?

6. In which country is the UNESCO World Heritage Site Himeji Castle located?

7. The Atocha Tropical Garden is a botanical garden within which city's main train station?

8. Which landmark in Egypt is a colossal statue with the body of a lion and the head of a pharaoh?

9. Nelson's Column is a monument on which London square?

10. Which island in New York harbour was home to an immigration station that, between 1892 and 1954, welcomed over 12 million people into the United States?

11. In which Spanish city is the Plaza de España located?

12. Famous for its jazz clubs, which US city is home to the historic French Quarter?

13. The Vasari Corridor is a 1km walkway connecting the Uffizi Gallery to the Pitti Palace. Over which bridge does it extend?

14. La Bombonera is a famous football stadium, home to Boca Juniors, located in which country?

15. The Acropolis is a famous historical site in which city?

16. The Dom Luís I Bridge is a double-deck arch bridge crossing the River Douro in which city?

17. Which London art gallery is housed in a former power station?

18. The Sphere is a music and entertainment arena that opened in 2023 in which US city?

19. The Cu Chi Tunnels are located in which country?

20. The Statue of Liberty was a gift to the United States from which country?

North America Geography - Quiz 2

Answers on page 226

1. What is the state capital of California?

2. The scenic *Going-to-the-Sun Road* is located in which state's Glacier National Park?

3. In which Canadian province is the city of Calgary located?

4. What is the largest island in the Caribbean?

5. Which is the only US State that has a name beginning with the letter F?

6. Mount Rushmore is located in which US state?

    a. North Dakota
    b. South Dakota
    c. Texas
    d. Wisconsin

7. Which US state is farthest west?

8. In which US state would you find Stone Mountain Park?

9. Pearson International Airport serves which North American city?

10. Frankenmuth, a city nicknamed *Little Bavaria*, is located in which state?

11. True or false: Mexico City has hosted the Summer Olympics?

12. What bay does the Golden Gate Strait lead into?

13. Goat Island divides what natural wonder on the border of Canada and the USA?

14. In 1871, the official addition of which province gave Canada coasts on both the Atlantic and the Pacific Oceans?

    a. British Columbia
    b. Alberta
    c. Newfoundland and Labrador
    d. New Brunswick

15. What US state has cities such as Flagstaff, Mesa, and Phoenix?

16. Which state is Mexico's largest state?

    a. Durango
    b. Chiapas
    c. Chihuahua
    d. Oaxaca

17. Which US city is home to sports teams called The Cubs, The Bears, and The Fire?

18. What desert valley is located in Eastern California?

19. In which US state is the world's most active volcano?

20. Which major river flows through New Orleans?

Oceania Geography - Quiz 2

Answers on page 226

1. Wallaman Falls is the highest single-drop waterfall in which country?

   a. Australia
   b. Papua New Guinea
   c. New Zealand
   d. Fiji

2. Adelaide is the capital of which Australian state?

3. What is the largest city on New Zealand's South Island?

4. What is the capital city of Tuvalu?

   a. Palikir
   b. Funafuti
   c. Suva
   d. Port Vila

5. What is the mountain range in New Zealand that spans much of the South Island?

a. Southern Andes

b. Southern Appalachians

c. Southern Alps

d. Southern Pennines

6. The Gordon Dam, the largest in Australia, is located in which state?

a. Victoria

b. South Australia

c. Queensland

d. Tasmania

7. What major rainforest covers a significant part of Papua New Guinea?

8. In which New Zealand city would you find a statue of *Pania*, a figure from Māori mythology?

a. Dunedin

b. Christchurch

c. Napier

d. Hamilton

9. Which city is home to Australia's tallest building?

10. What island chain in Papua New Guinea is known for volcanic activity?

    a. Nassau Archipelago
    b. Bismarck Archipelago
    c. Kaiser Archipelago
    d. König Archipelago

11. How many deserts are there in Australia?

    a. 0
    b. 2
    c. 5
    d. 10

12. Which river is the longest in Australia?

13. What is the approximate population of New Zealand?

    a. 5 million
    b. 10 million
    c. 20 million

d. 30 million

14. What is the name of the vast, dry region in central Australia?

15. What type of climate does Samoa experience?

16. Which Pacific island nation is known for its underwater post office?

    a. Vanuatu
    b. Fiji
    c. Tuvalu
    d. Samoa

17. What is the approximate population of Australia?

    a. 15 million
    b. 25 million
    c. 35 million
    d. 50 million

18. The Socceroos is the nickname for which country's national football team?

19. What is the capital city of Papua New
    Guinea?

20. Which island, which is an Australian
    territory, is nicknamed the *Galapagos of the
    Indian Ocean*?

Rivers, Seas & Oceans - Quiz 2

Answers on page 227

1. Which natural lake is the largest in England by surface area?

2. On which continent is the Orinoco River?

3. By area, what is the smallest ocean in the world?

4. Jalisco, located near the city of Guadalajara, is home to Mexico's largest freshwater lake. What is it called?

   a. Lake Chapala
   b. Lake Guadalajara
   c. Lake Magdalena
   d. Lake Texcoco

5. What is the name of the world's highest uninterrupted waterfall?

6. Which strait separates Sri Lanka from India?

7. The Rio Grande forms the border between Mexico and which US state?

8. What is the longest river in Colombia?

    a. Magdalena
    b. Amazon
    c. Caño Cristales
    d. Salado

9. What canal connects the Red Sea to the Mediterranean Sea?

10. The Victoria Falls are located on which major river in Africa?

11. The Okavango Delta, one of the world's largest inland deltas, is located in which African country?

    a. South Africa
    b. Zimbabwe
    c. Rwanda
    d. Botswana

12. The 27 waterfalls of Damajagua are located in which Caribbean country?

a. Antigua and Barbuda

b. Dominican Republic

c. St. Lucia

d. Jamaica

13. What is the longest river in Spain?

a. Minho

b. Bidasoa

c. Tagus

d. Llobregat

14. Which major river flows through Turkey and forms part of its southern border with Syria?

15. Porto is situated along the banks of which river?

16. On its east, the New Zealand city of Auckland touches the Pacific Ocean. What is the body of water that borders Auckland to its west?

17. What is the deepest river in the world?

a. Amazon

b. Congo

c. Nile

d. Yangtze

18. Which river splits the city of Budapest into
    its two sides, Buda and Pest?

19. The Three Gorges Dam is a hydroelectric
    gravity dam in China spanning which river?

20. Located on the Lucala River, which country is
    home to Kalandula Falls, one of Africa's
    largest falls?

    a. Angola
    b. Democratic Republic of the Congo
    c. Ivory Coast
    d. Burkina Faso

South America Geography - Quiz 2

Answers on page 228

1. What is the name of the highest point on the
   Inca Trail, the road leading to Machu Picchu?

   a. The Andean Drop
   b. Dead Woman's Pass
   c. Sun Gate
   d. Pizarro Pass

2. Which South American capital city is home
   to the archaeological Museum of Gold?

3. The driest non-polar desert in the world, the
   Atacama Desert is located in which country?

4. Which of the following countries does NOT
   share a border with Peru?

   a. Bolivia
   b. Uruguay
   c. Ecuador
   d. Chile

5. What is the only South American country to have hosted the Olympic Games?

6. What is the capital city of Uruguay?

7. The Andean city of Cusco is located in which country?

    a. Bolivia
    b. Colombia
    c. Ecuador
    d. Peru

8. The cities of Asunción and San Lorenzo can be found in which country?

9. Best known for being the home of the gauchos, The Pampas is a vast plain in which country?

10. What is the name of the famous endangered big cat that roams the Amazon rainforest?

11. What is Brazil's main agricultural export?

    a. Beef
    b. Brazil Nuts

c. Soybeans

d. Avocados

12. What type of bear is the only bear native to South America?

13. Copacabana is a famous beach in which city?

14. *The Altiplano* is a high plateau in South America, primarily located in which country?

a. Argentina
b. Bolivia
c. Paraguay
d. Uruguay

15. Peru is known for which of these mountains?

a. Prism Mountain
b. Pyramid Mountain
c. Rainbow Mountain
d. Bow Mountain

16. What is the official currency of Colombia?

17. Aconcagua is the highest peak in which mountain range?

18. The westernmost point in mainland South America is Punta Pariñas. Which country is this in?

19. What is the population of Chile?

   a. 5 million
   b. 10 million
   c. 20 million
   d. 40 million

20. *Los Pumas* is the nickname for which country's national rugby union team?

Sports Geography - Quiz 2

Answers on page 229

1. *The Silver Ferns* is the nickname for which country's women's netball team?

2. In which country would you find Pebble Beach golf course?

    a. Canada
    b. UK
    c. USA
    d. Australia

3. Which famous Portuguese footballer was born in Madeira and has the international airport there named after him?

4. What is the name of the iconic cricket stadium in Cape Town which is set in the foothills of Table Mountain?

5. In which US state do the New York Giants and New York Jets play their home games?

6. What is Japan's official national sport?

7. The Kaizer Chiefs is a football team, giving inspiration to the band Kaiser Chiefs, based in which country?

    a. UK
    b. New Zealand
    c. South Africa
    d. Mali

8. The 2002 Winter Olympics were held in which US city?

9. Pato is a sport played on horseback, combining elements from polo and basketball. Which South American country is Pato the national sport of?

10. Which sport do the Boston Red Sox and Chicago White Sox play?

11. What is the largest-capacity football stadium in Europe?

    a. Wembley Stadium
    b. Camp Nou
    c. San Siro

d. Stade de France

12. *The Fight of the Century* between
    Muhammad Ali and Joe Frazier, which Frazier
    won, took place where?

    a. Kinshasa
    b. New York City
    c. Las Vegas
    d. Manila

13. At over 4,300m above sea level, which
    country is home to the highest altitude
    sports stadium in the world?

    a. South Africa
    b. Bolivia
    c. Peru
    d. Switzerland

14. The Rod Laver Arena is home to which major
    tennis tournament?

15. Due to its slow average speed, which
    Formula One track is the shortest race on the
    F1 calendar?

16. Rugby Union is the de facto national sport of
    which of these countries?

    a. Brazil
    b. Madagascar
    c. Ethiopia
    d. Sri Lanka

17. Which country hosted the 1998 FIFA World
    Cup?

18. The Galaxy, The Rams, and The Raiders
    represent which US city in their respective
    sports?

19. The Solheim Cup is a competition between
    teams representing Europe and the USA.
    Which sport is it?

20. Lambeau Field, home to Green Bay Packers,
    typically plays host to which sport?

United Kingdom Geography - Quiz 2

Answers on page 230

1. Which of these Scottish islands is known as
    the Queen of the Hebrides?

    a. Islay
    b. Skye
    c. Mull
    d. Arran

2. What is the only city in Cornwall?

3. In which national park would you find
    Helvellyn?

4. What is the longest motorway in the UK?

5. Which city's airport is named after John
    Lennon?

6. What is the tallest mountain in the UK?

7. What's the northernmost island in the UK?

8. In which London park is London Zoo
    situated?

9. Which county is Leeds Castle in?

10. The supposed birthplace of King Arthur,
    Tintagel Castle is in which English county?

11. Which seaside town is home to the world's
    longest pleasure pier?

12. What is the largest national park in the UK?

13. In which city is the National Railway
    Museum?

14. Which river flows through Dundee?

15. Which city's airport has the IATA code NWI?

16. In which county is the theme park Alton
    Towers located?

17. Which Scottish city is nicknamed *The
    Granite City*?

18. What is the name of Birmingham's iconic
     shopping centre, known for its futuristic
     architecture and the Selfridges building?

19. What northeast seaside town is home to the
     dining and leisure centre The Spanish City?

20. In which city would you find Temple Meads
     railway station?

World Geography - Quiz 3

Answers on page 231

1. Which bay of the Indian Ocean is the largest
    bay in the world?

2. Grand Mesa in Colorado is the world's
    largest what?

    a. Vertical Cliff
    b. Flat-Top Mountain
    c. Canyon
    d. Salt Flat

3. What is the second largest rainforest in the
    world?

4. What is the official language of
    Guadeloupe?

5. What is the only continent where meerkats
    can be seen in the wild?

6. What is considered to be the world's oldest
    desert?

7. Taller than Table Mountain and Mount Snowdon, Duna Federico Kirbus is the largest sand dune in the world at 1230 metres. In which country is it located?

   a. Argentina
   b. Peru
   c. Namibia
   d. South Africa

8. Known for its annual Apple Blossom Festival, the Annapolis Valley is located in which country?

   a. New Zealand
   b. Canada
   c. USA
   d. Sweden

9. What is the name of the strait that separates Turkey's Asian and European parts?

10. What is the world's shallowest ocean?

   a. Arctic
   b. Indian
   c. Southern

d. Atlantic

11. Moon Valley (Valley de la Luna) is home to a moonlike landscape, featuring dunes, rugged mountains, and distinctive rock formations. Which country is it in?

a. Chile
b. Portugal
c. Spain
d. Mexico

12. What is the longest river on Earth?

13. Measuring 132 miles, *Casino Beach* is the world's longest uninterrupted sea beach. Which country is it in?

a. Brazil
b. Australia
c. India
d. Canada

14. Which city is home to the largest parliament building in the world?

15. Acapulco was once a popular party town, with the likes of Frank Sinatra and Elvis Presley frequenting it, on which country's Pacific coast?

16. Where is the hottest place on Earth?

17. Oktoberfest is a large, annual beer festival that takes place in which city?

18. What is the longest road in the world?

   a. Pan-American Highway
   b. Trans-Canada Highway
   c. Trans-Siberian Highway
   d. Route 66

19. Which country has the most islands in the world?

   a. Croatia
   b. Indonesia
   c. Maldives
   d. Sweden

20. Carved by Snake River, what is the deepest canyon in North America?

a. Grand Canyon
b. Hells Canyon
c. Bighorn Canyon
d. Desolation Canyon

Africa Geography - Quiz 3

Answers on page 232

1. What tree is the national tree of
   Madagascar?

   a. Willow
   b. Baobab
   c. Palm
   d. Mopane

2. Approximately ten times the size of the UK,
   what is the biggest country by area in Africa?

3. What currency is used in Nigeria?

   a. Franc
   b. Dollar
   c. Naira
   d. Pound

4. Which country is NOT located in North
   Africa?

   a. Libya
   b. Benin
   c. Tunisia

d. Egypt

5. With over 130,000 elephants living within its boundaries, which African country is home to the world's largest elephant population?

6. Overlooking Camps Bay, the Twelve Apostles is a mountain range in which city?

7. What is the official language of Mozambique?

8. The city of Abidjan is located in which West African country?

9. Mumbo Island is a pristine and deserted tropical island floating on the expansive waters of which African Great Lake?

    a. Lake Victoria
    b. Lake Malawi
    c. Lake Turkana
    d. Lake Albert

10. Kampala is the capital city of which landlocked African country?

a. Lesotho

b. Uganda

c. Zambia

d. Burkina Faso

11. In which country is the ancient city of
    Timbuktu located?

    a. Chad

    b. Zambia

    c. Mali

    d. Central African Republic

12. Which African country has the largest
    population?

13. The Nile River is formed by the confluence of
    the White Nile and the Blue Nile. In which
    capital city do these two rivers meet?

    a. Cairo

    b. Khartoum

    c. Tripoli

    d. Algiers

14. Which West African country is home to the famous *Slave Coast* and has the capital city of Lomé?

15. The Congo River is the second-longest river in Africa. In which country does the river flow primarily?

16. Luanda is a port city and the capital city of which country on the Atlantic coast of Africa?

    a. Angola
    b. Namibia
    c. Mauritania
    d. Senegal

17. What is the name of the national park in South Africa that is home to the *Big Five* (lion, leopard, rhinoceros, elephant, and buffalo)?

18. In which North African country can you find the ancient Roman ruins of Volubilis?

19. What is the smallest country on continental Africa?

a. The Gambia

b. Equatorial Guinea

c. Burundi

d. Togo

20. Known as the *City of Gold*, what is the largest city in South Africa by population?

Asia Geography - Quiz 3

Answers on page 233

1. Negombo, Galle, and Kandy are all cities in which country?

2. The Caspian Sea borders several countries in Central Asia. Which two "Stans" are located on its shores?

3. What is the official currency of India?

4. The Shinano River is the longest river in which country?

   a. Malaysia
   b. Taiwan
   c. Japan
   d. South Korea

5. What is the capital city of Pakistan?

   a. Islamabad
   b. Karachi
   c. Lahore
   d. Faisalabad

6. Which city is the financial and economic hub of China and is located on the East China Sea?

7. What is the official language of Bangladesh?

8. Busan and Daegu are cities in which country?

9. Which two countries share the shores of the Dead Sea?

10. Which Japanese city was the site of the first atomic bombing in history during World War II?

11. Which mountain range forms the northern boundary of India?

12. Iran shares its northern border with which large body of water?

13. Which Southeast Asian country shares a border with both China and Vietnam?

14. Which city in India is known as the *Pink City*, due to its buildings being painted in a rosy

terracotta colour? The city was painted pink in 1876 to welcome Queen Victoria and the Prince of Wales.

15. Hong Kong to which city represents the busiest flight route in the world, with more than 571,000 seats available each month?

    a. Singapore
    b. Taipei
    c. Dubai
    d. Shanghai

16. What is the approximate population of Vietnam?

    a. 20 million
    b. 40 million
    c. 70 million
    d. 100 million

17. What is Japan's national flower?

18. Which river flows through Bangkok?

19. Which city in India was formerly known as
     Madras?

20. Which Southeast Asian country is home to
     the famous rice terraces of Banaue?

Capital Cities - Quiz 3

Answers on page 234

1. Which capital city hosted the 2004 Olympics?

2. What is the capital city of Malta?

3. What is the capital city of Mauritania?

   a. Bamako
   b. Nouakchott
   c. Dakar
   d. Rabat

4. Sitting 28 metres below sea level, what is the lowest-lying capital city in the world?

5. What is the capital city of Switzerland?

6. Which capital city is home to districts such as Shibuya and Shinjuku?

7. What is the capital city of Belarus?

8. What is the capital city of Turkmenistan?

a. Tashkent

b. Baku

c. Dushanbe

d. Ashgabat

9. Which capital city is home to Tiananmen Square?

10. What is the capital city of Georgia?

11. Which capital city is home to the football team DC United?

12. What is the capital city of Iran?

13. What is the least populated capital city in the world?

a. Ngerulmud, Palau

b. Suva, Fiji

c. Andorra la Vella, Andorra

d. Thimphu, Bhutan

14. Which country changed its capital city from Tselinograd to Astana in 1997?

15. Riga is the capital of which country?

    a. Latvia
    b. Lithuania
    c. Estonia
    d. Finland

16. Which capital city was built on seven hills,
     including the Palatine Hill?

17. What is the capital city of Mali?

    a. Accra
    b. Bamako
    c. Ouagadougou
    d. Tripoli

18. What is the capital city of Botswana?

    a. Gaborone
    b. Luanda
    c. Lusaka
    d. Harare

19. What is the world's southernmost capital
     city?

20. Which capital city is home to attractions such as Fisherman's Bastion and Heroes' Square?

Europe Geography - Quiz 3

Answers on page 234

1. The Ponte Vecchio is a mediaeval bridge in what Italian city?

2. Cantabria is a region of which European country?

3. What is the largest Greek island?

4. On what Mediterranean island would you find Cape Carbonara?

5. What country is Krka National Park in?

6. The largest lake in Eastern Europe, Lake Balaton, is situated in which country?

7. In which Spanish city would you find Plaza de España?

8. The Silver Coast is located in which European country?

9. Belek is a resort town on the Mediterranean coast of which country?

10. In which city is Europe's largest synagogue located?

11. In which French city can you visit the Cité du Vin wine museum?

12. What are the three countries that make up the Baltic States?

13. What is the name of the mountain range that forms the southern border of Poland?

14. Which Swiss lake is the largest in the country and shared with France?

15. Tenerife is Spain's largest island by population. What is the second largest?

16. Which city is home to Anne Frank House?

17. In which city can you visit the Doge's Palace?

18. In which city can you walk across the
     Charles Bridge?

19. What is the largest lake in Italy?

20. Which UK royal castle is the largest
     occupied castle in the world?

     a. Balmoral Castle
     b. Windsor Castle
     c. Warwick Castle
     d. Stirling Castle

Guess the Country - Quiz 3

Answers on page 235

1. Which country is this?

    a. Italy
    b. Bolivia
    c. Peru
    d. Angola

2. Which country is this?

    a. France
    b. Germany
    c. Romania
    d. Ireland

3. Which country is this?

    a. China
    b. Canada
    c. Mongolia
    d. USA

4. Which country is this?

   a. Estonia
   b. Somalia
   c. Argentina
   d. New Zealand

5. Which country is this?

   a. Belgium
   b. Venezuela
   c. Barbados
   d. Brazil

6. Which country is this?

   a. Sri Lanka
   b. Fiji
   c. Malta
   d. Taiwan

7. Which country is this?

   a. Chile
   b. Benin
   c. Myanmar
   d. Portugal

8. Which country is this?

   a. The Gambia
   b. Ivory Coast
   c. Ecuador
   d. Cape Verde

9. Which country is this?

   a. Jamaica
   b. Cuba
   c. Madagascar
   d. St. Lucia

10. Which country is this?

    a. Thailand
    b. Vietnam
    c. Japan
    d. South Korea

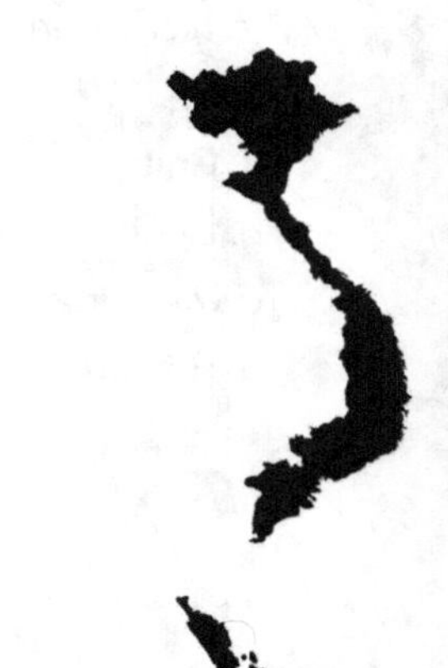

11. Which country is this?

    a. Japan
    b. New Zealand
    c. The Bahamas
    d. Samoa

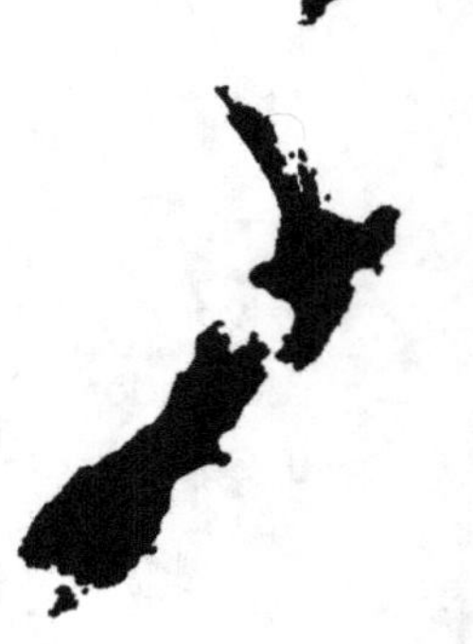

12. Which country is this?

    a. Niger
    b. Chad
    c. Egypt
    d. Sudan

13. Which country is this?

   a. Qatar
   b. Bahrain
   c. United Arab Emirates
   d. Saudi Arabia

14. Which country is this?

   a. The Netherlands
   b. Belgium
   c. Bangladesh
   d. Mauritius

15. Which country is this?

   a. Norway
   b. Sweden
   c. Finland
   d. Lithuania

16. Which country is this?

    a. Hungary
    b. Austria
    c. Czech Republic
    d. Ukraine

17. Which country is this?

    a. Iceland
    b. Denmark
    c. Cyprus
    d. Malta

18. Which country is this?

    a. Mauritania
    b. Republic of the Congo
    c. Namibia
    d. Gabon

19. Which country is this?

a. Papua New Guinea
b. Malaysia
c. The Philippines
d. Japan

20. Which country is this?

a. Tuvalu
b. Chile
c. Cuba
d. Sweden

North America Geography - Quiz 3

Answers on page 236

1. Which world famous landmark is found on Mount Lee?

2. Roxbury, Dorchester and Beacon Hill are neighbourhoods of which city?

   a. Atlanta
   b. Boston
   c. Chicago
   d. Los Angeles

3. Which Florida city is home to Ocean Drive and South Beach?

4. Which US state does Tijuana in Mexico share a border with?

5. What is the easternmost Canadian province?

6. Which US state is home to Augusta National Golf Club, where the Masters takes place every year?

7. Costa Rica has coastlines on two bodies of
    water. Which coast is longer: the Pacific or
    the Caribbean?

8. When measured from the ocean floor,
    Mauna Kea is the tallest mountain in the
    world. Where is it located?

9. Established in 1872, which US national park
    was the world's first?

    a. Yosemite
    b. Redwood
    c. Yellowstone
    d. Everglades

10. Which US city is often referred to as *Music
    City*?

11. Used for land speed racing, the Bonneville
    Salt Flats are located in which US state?

12. Sangster International Airport in Montego
    Bay serves which Caribbean island?

13. In which US city can you go up The Space
     Needle observation tower?

14. Approximately how many times larger than
     the UK is the state of Texas?

     a. 2 times
     b. 3 times
     c. 5 times
     d. 10 times

15. Which of these US states does NOT have an
     Atlantic coastline?

     a. Maine
     b. New Jersey
     c. Florida
     d. West Virginia

16. Hurricane Katrina struck New Orleans and
     its surrounding area in what year?

17. Sacramento is the capital of which US state?

18. Which lake is NOT found in Canada?

     a. Lake Huron

b. Lake Superior

c. Great Salt Lake

d. Lake Ontario

19. In which US state is the Lake of the Ozarks
    located?

    a. Idaho

    b. Nebraska

    c. Missouri

    d. Ohio

20. Which of the following is a city in Nova
    Scotia in Canada?

    a. Barclays

    b. Halifax

    c. Natwest

    d. Santander

Oceania Geography - Quiz 3

Answers on page 237

1. What is the national sport of Samoa?

2. Which mountain range runs along the east coast of Australia?

3. Which city in Australia is often dubbed The Harbour City?

4. DUD is the IATA code for which New Zealand airport?

5. Fremantle in Western Australia was historically which city's sister city?

6. Barossa Valley in South Australia is a wine region renowned for producing which type of wine?

7. What is the name of the volcano in New Zealand that erupted in 2019, causing a significant disaster?

8. What is the name of the famous large rock formation in central Australia?

9. What is the name of the largest bay in Australia?

   a. Crocodile Bay
   b. Shark Bay
   c. Koala Bay
   d. Kangaroo Bay

10. The Echo Point Lookout offers a great view of The Three Sisters. In which New South Wales mountain range can you visit the lookout?

11. True or false: Perth is closer to Bali than it is to Canberra?

12. Which city is the capital of the state of Queensland?

13. Which island in New Zealand is known for its geothermal activity, including geysers and hot springs?

14. What is the capital city of Tonga?

    a. Apia
    b. Suva
    c. Nukuʻalofa
    d. Tarawa

15. Cairns is a city in which Australian state?

16. NAN is the IATA code for the international airport on which Pacific Island country?

17. What is the national sport of Papua New Guinea?

18. Which city is the capital of the state of Victoria?

19. What is the national animal of Australia?

20. Which city in Australia will host the Summer Olympics in 2032?

Rivers, Seas & Oceans - Quiz 3

Answers on page 238

1. The Amazon River is the longest in South America, but what is the second-longest river in South America?

2. In which ocean can you find the 25,000 mile line of volcanic activity known as the Ring of Fire?

3. What is the only ocean that blue whales do NOT inhabit?

4. What word beginning with *A* means a ring-shaped reef of coral that completely encloses a lagoon?

5. The global intersection of zero degrees latitude and zero degrees longitude is found in which ocean?

6. Which river flows through Nottingham in the UK?

7. What is the deepest part of the Atlantic Ocean?

a. South Sandwich Trench

b. Puerto Rico Trench

c. Romanche Trench

d. Cape Verde Trench

8. Luzon is the biggest and most populated island in what archipelago country in the western Pacific Ocean?

9. The Ever Given container ship blocked which major shipping canal for 6 days in 2021?

10. The Labrador Sea is a marginal sea of which ocean?

11. What is the UK's shortest river at just 800 metres long?

a. River Ness

b. River Morar

c. River Leven

d. River Ely

12. Which ocean is the warmest on average?

13. Lake Ladoga, the largest lake in Europe, is located in which country?

    a. Slovenia
    b. Germany
    c. Switzerland
    d. Russia

14. Skagerrak is a strait connecting the Baltic Sea to which other sea of the Atlantic Ocean?

15. Which major river passes through Vienna, Bratislava, Budapest, and Belgrade?

16. How many lakes make up the Great Lakes in North America?

17. Which river in Illinois is dyed green every year in celebration of St. Patrick's Day?

18. By water volume, which country has the largest waterfall in Europe?

    a. Norway
    b. Switzerland

c. Iceland

d. UK

19. Which river flows through Amsterdam?

20. Which ocean has the most islands?

South America Geography - Quiz 3

Answers on page 239

1. Home to over 1,200 wineries, also known as bodegas, Mendoza produces around two-thirds of which country's wine?

2. What is the second-largest city in Colombia?

3. The Itaipu Dam is considered one of the seven modern wonders of the world. It's situated on the Paraná River on the border between Brazil and which other country?

4. Carrasco International Airport is the main airport in which country?

5. Which country in Central America borders Colombia to the north?

6. In which country is South America's tallest building, the Gran Torre Santiago, located?

7. Which country in South America is the world's biggest producer of coffee?

8. River Plate and Boca Juniors are popular
    football teams in which country?

9. Which country is home to Angel Falls?

10. The art of weaving the traditional toquilla
    hat, also known as the Panama hat, was
    added to the UNESCO Intangible Cultural
    Heritage Lists in 2012. In which country do
    these hats originate?

11. The Guajira Peninsula is the northernmost
    point in South America. Which country is it
    in?

12. Which country is nicknamed *Land of Silver*
    after a Venetian explorer working for Spain
    went there in the 1520s in search of the
    precious metal?

13. The world's largest salt flat, the Uyuni Salt
    Flat, is located in which country?

14. The biggest earthquake ever recorded, of
    magnitude 9.5, happened in 1960, at a
    subduction zone where the Pacific plate
    dives under the South American plate.

Which country did it hit?

15. What food crop did the Spanish bring back
to Europe from Peru when they were digging
for silver and gold in the 1500s?

16. La Plata, Salta, and Rosario are cities in
which country?

17. What is the smallest country in South
America?

18. What is the approximate population of Peru?

a. 4 million
b. 14 million
c. 24 million
d. 34 million

19. The state of Mato Grosso, the state of
Paraná, and the state of Bahia are states in
which country?

20. *Los Cafeteros* is the nickname for which
men's national football team, so called for
their country's coffee production?

Sports Geography - Quiz 3

Answers on page 240

1. Which sport is considered to be the national sport of the USA?

2. At which venue in London is the PDC World Darts Championship held each year?

3. Grasshoppers and Young Boys are football teams from which country?

   a. Turkey
   b. Italy
   c. Switzerland
   d. Austria

4. Which city has the most sports stadiums in the world?

5. Which country is former tennis player Steffi Graff from?

6. What is the national sport of Italy?

7. Which English rugby union team play their rugby at The Recreation Ground?

a. Leicester Tigers

b. Northampton Saints

c. Bath Rugby

d. Saracens

8. Which sport does Spaniard Sergio Garcia play?

9. AC Milan and which other club share the same home ground of the San Siro?

10. Wrigley Field and Fenway Park are famous stadiums in which sport?

11. Rugby player Keith Wood represented which country?

12. What is the national sport of China?

13. The fast growing sport Padel is thought to have originated in which country?

a. Mexico

b. USA

c. Portugal

d. Argentina

14. Which football club changed the name of
their stadium from Stadio San Paolo to
Stadio Diego Armando Maradona in honour
of their former player?

15. Playing at the Rogers Centre, the Blue Jays
are a baseball team in which major North
American city?

16. The America's Cup is the oldest international
trophy in world sport. Which sport is it?

17. Don Bradman is widely regarded as the best
batsman of all time. For which country did he
play cricket?

18. What is the national sport of Turkey?

a. Football
b. Oil Wrestling
c. Weightlifting
d. Volleyball

19. Which English football team play their home
    games at The Stadium of Light?

20. Ayrton Senna, one of the greatest ever
    Formula One drivers, was from which
    country?

United Kingdom Geography - Quiz 3

Answers on page 240

1. Which county is credited with the invention of the pork pie?

2. Canary Wharf is in which London borough?

3. In which English county is Sherwood Forest?

4. What is the second-highest mountain in the UK?

   a. Snowdon
   b. Scafell Pike
   c. Braeriach
   d. Ben Macdui

5. Glyndebourne Opera House is in which county?

6. Tynwald Day is a public holiday on which Island?

7. In which English city can you visit the National Football Museum?

8. Campbeltown, Highland, Islay, Lowland and Speyside are the 5 regions in Scotland that produce what?

9. Whitby and Robin Hood's Bay are coastal towns within which national park?

10. Which line on the London Underground connects London Bridge to King's Cross & St Pancras International?

11. Which county is the market town Maidenhead in?

12. Portstewart and Portrush are small towns in which country of the UK?

13. Which city in the UK has the IV postcode?

14. The M62 motorway passes through which range of uplands?

15. On which motorway is the Spaghetti Junction?

16. In which city would you find the Titanic
     Museum?

17. What is the name of the strait that separates
     the Isle of Wight from mainland England?

18. Liverpool is located on the banks of which
     river?

19.   Which county is Harrogate in?

20. What is the name of the historic street in
     Edinburgh that runs from Edinburgh Castle
     to the Palace of Holyroodhouse?

World Geography - Quiz 4

Answers on page 241

1. What is the longest railway in the world?

2. Which village is located on the north coast of Tristan da Cunha in the South Atlantic Ocean and is considered to be the most remote settlement in the world?

   a. London of the Seven Seas
   b. Edinburgh of the Seven Seas
   c. Belfast of the Seven Seas
   d. Cardiff of the Seven Seas

3. What country was the Caesar Salad invented in?

4. Which country was the first in the world to use paper money?

   a. UK
   b. France
   c. China
   d. Finland

5. Samsung, one of the world's largest manufacturers of electronic devices, was founded in which country?

6. Alice Springs is a remote town in the outback of Australia, halfway between Darwin and Adelaide. Which region of Australia is it in?

7. Asian and African elephants differ in several ways. Which of the two have smaller ears?

8. In which sea is Aruba located?

9. In which US state is the Grand Canyon located?

10. What is the world's smallest sea?

    a. Sea of Marmara
    b. Labrador Sea
    c. Baltic Sea
    d. Sea of Azov

11. What is the northernmost capital city in the world?

12. In which ocean is the Bermuda Triangle located?

13. Napa Valley is a famous wine region in which country?

14. Which country has the larger population: Colombia or Morocco?

15. In which country would you find Lake Louise?

16. What's the capital city of India?

17. The Marble Caves on the edge of General Carrera Lake are a mesmerising sight of pure marble columns that have been carved out over thousands of years. Where are they located?

a. Spain
b. Italy
c. Chile
d. Norway

18. Which city does LaGuardia Airport serve?

19. What is the southernmost state in the USA?

   a. Florida
   b. Hawaii
   c. Texas
   d. California

20. The Pinnacles Desert in Nambung National Park is well known for its limestone structures that rise from the golden sand. These lunar-like pillars were created from the sea receding that left behind deposits of sea shells 25,000 - 30,000 years ago. Which country is the desert in?

   a. USA
   b. South Africa
   c. Australia
   d. Mexico

Africa Geography - Quiz 4

Answers on page 242

1. Which of these is NOT a city in Morocco?

    a. Rabat
    b. Casablanca
    c. Oran
    d. Tangier

2. The Jomo Kenyatta International Airport serves which African capital city?

3. With close to 250 pyramids, which African country has the most pyramids in the world?

    a. Egypt
    b. Sudan
    c. Libya
    d. Algeria

4. Which metal is Zambia's biggest export?

    a. Gold
    b. Copper
    c. Silver

d. Aluminium

5. What is the national animal of South Africa?

6. Which country was formerly known as Rhodesia?

7. True or false: no giraffes live in Tanzania?

8. The extinct flightless bird the dodo was endemic to which island nation in the Indian Ocean?

   a. Maldives
   b. Comoros
   c. Mauritius
   d. Seychelles

9. Standing at 400 metres, the Iconic Tower is the tallest building in Africa. Where is it?

   a. Egypt
   b. South Africa
   c. Nigeria
   d. Tunisia

10. Which of these is NOT a city in South Africa?

    a. Durban
    b. Windhoek
    c. Bloemfontein
    d. Pretoria

11. Uganda has two official languages with one
     being English. What is the other?

    a. French
    b. Swahili
    c. Portuguese
    d. Zulu

12. The Piton de la Fournaise is one of the most
     active volcanoes in the world. On which
     Indian Ocean island is it located?

    a. Madagascar
    b. Réunion
    c. Christmas Island
    d. Maldives

13. Robben Island, just off the coast of Cape
     Town, was famously used for what purpose?

a. Penguin Sanctuary

b. Prison

c. Army Base

d. Astronomy

14. Which country in Africa is the world's largest cocoa producer?

    a. Uganda

    b. Ivory Coast

    c. Mozambique

    d. Liberia

15. Which animal is Kenya's Lake Nakuru National Park famous for?

    a. Rhino

    b. Elephant

    c. Flamingo

    d. Hippo

16. Which country borders Angola to the north?

    a. Democratic Republic of the Congo

    b. Namibia

    c. Central African Republic

d. Equatorial Guinea

17. What currency is used in Somalia?

    a. Somali Dollar
    b. Somali Pound
    c. Somali Shilling
    d. Somali Cedi

18. Which country produces 40% of Africa's coffee?

    a. Kenya
    b. Senegal
    c. Zimbabwe
    d. Ethiopia

19. The Kariba Dam formed Lake Kariba, which is the largest man-made lake in the world. Located in Zimbabwe, along which river is the dam?

    a. Zambezi River
    b. Limpopo River
    c. Congo River
    d. Cubango River

20. Which country in Africa has the largest
     concentration of animals per square mile in
     the world?

Asia Geography - Quiz 4

Answers on page 243

1. What did Ceylon change its name to in 1972?

2. What side of the road do vehicles drive on in Japan?

3. What type of transport is the Shanghai Maglev?

4. VinWonders is a theme park in which country?

   a. Vietnam
   b. Malaysia
   c. South Korea
   d. Indonesia

5. Which famous Indian landmark is situated on the banks of the River Yamuna in the city of Agra?

6. Vissel Kobe in Japan play which sport?

7. What is the official currency of Indonesia?

    a. Peso
    b. Rupiah
    c. Dollar
    d. Yen

8. Which Asian country is nicknamed *The Land of the Thunder Dragon*?

    a. Sri Lanka
    b. Bhutan
    c. Laos
    d. Japan

9. What is the only species of bear native to China?

10. Which country has the larger population: Pakistan or Bangladesh?

11. Which of these is NOT a city in Vietnam?

    a. Hanoi
    b. Hue
    c. Yangon

d. Nha Trang

12. What is the capital city of Nepal?

13. Bangladesh's flag features a red circle on what colour background?

14. What is Japan's tallest mountain?

15. The Kandawgyi Lake, also known as Royal Lake, is an artificial lake that was constructed by the British. It's one of two major lakes in the capital city of which Southeast Asian country?

a. Malaysia
b. Thailand
c. Myanmar
d. Vietnam

16. Which tropical fruit, often associated with India and Southeast Asia, is considered the national fruit of several countries, including India?

17. There are 3 Disneyland theme parks located in Asia. There is one in Tokyo and one in

Hong Kong. Where is the third located?

a. Taipei

b. Singapore

c. Shanghai

d. Shenzhen

18. Which small Asian country is famous for *momo*, a type of dumpling?

    a. Laos

    b. South Korea

    c. Nepal

    d. Taiwan

19. Which country is Asia's largest coffee producer, exporting about 1.5 million tonnes each year?

20. Which major Indian city was formerly known as Bombay?

Europe Geography - Quiz 4

Answers on page 244

1. On which island is the ancient city of Knossos located, considered to be the oldest city in Europe?

2. Which of these is NOT a city in Spain?

   a. Getafe
   b. Zaragoza
   c. Vigo
   d. Braga

3. In which country was the first Legoland theme park built?

4. In which German city is the headquarters of Volkswagen?

5. Europe and Asia are divided by which mountain range?

   a. Ural Mountains
   b. Caucasus Mountains
   c. Tatra Mountains

d. Carpathian Mountains

6. What is the largest island in the Mediterranean Sea?

7. In which city is the Sagrada Família located?

8. Which country has the larger population: Sweden or Denmark?

9. In which European country was the supermarket chain Aldi started?

10. Leonardo da Vinci–Fiumicino Airport serves which European city?

11. Pamukkale is a Turkish town known for its thermal waters that flow over white travertine terraces. Where is Pamukkale?

    a. Turkey
    b. Finland
    c. Italy
    d. Greece

12. In which city can you find *The Church of the Saviour on Spilled Blood*, a Russian

Orthodox church?

13. The Alster lakes are artificial lakes formed by the Alster River and located in the city centre of which German city?

14. Which of these is NOT a city in Italy?

    a. Brindisi
    b. Catania
    c. Foggia
    d. Tirana

15. What's the capital city of Denmark?

16. Ulm Minster in the city of Ulm is the tallest church building in the world. Which European country is Ulm in?

    a. Belgium
    b. Germany
    c. France
    d. Sweden

17. What is the name of the main square in Venice, Italy, famous for its basilica and

pigeons?

18. Which city is home to the largest port in Europe, handling more than 438 million tonnes of cargo per year?

19. Which of these is NOT a city in Belgium?

    a. Antwerp
    b. Dunkirk
    c. Ghent
    d. Brussels

20. Which country has the larger population: Spain or Italy?

Guess the Country - Quiz 4

Answers on page 245

1. Which country is this?

    a. Germany

    b. Bolivia

    c. France

    d. Spain

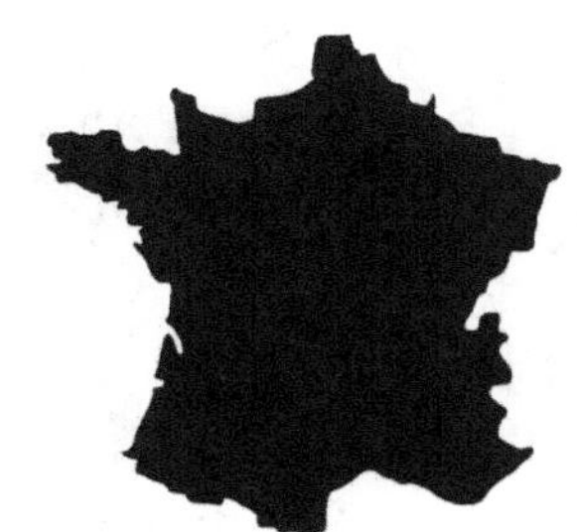

2. Which country is this?

    a. Croatia

    b. Mexico

    c. Samoa

    d. Thailand

3. Which country is this?

    a. Argentina

    b. China

    c. India

    d. Burundi

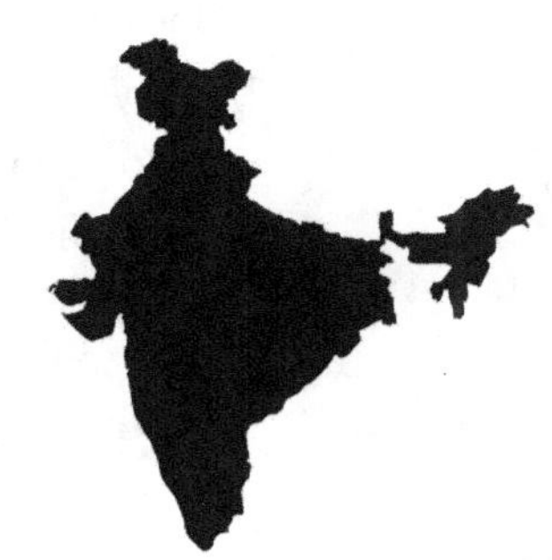

4. Which country is this?

   a. Denmark
   b. Sweden
   c. The Netherlands
   d. Belgium

5. Which country is this?

   a. Russia
   b. Turkey
   c. Brazil
   d. Australia

6. Which country is this?

   a. Japan
   b. Cuba
   c. Indonesia
   d. The Bahamas

7. Which country is this?

   a. Italy
   b. Georgia
   c. Sao Tome and Principe
   d. Luxembourg

8. Which country is this?

   a. Barbados
   b. Malta
   c. Cyprus
   d. Maldives

9. Which country is this?

   a. South Africa
   b. Algeria
   c. Romania
   d. Belarus

10.   Which country is this?

    a. Madagascar
    b. Sri Lanka
    c. Ireland
    d. Peru

11.   Which country is this?

    a. Argentina
    b. Liberia
    c. Guatemala
    d. French Guiana

12.   Which country is this?

    a. Libya
    b. Austria
    c. Estonia
    d. Canada

13.   Which country is this?

     a. Vietnam
     b. North Korea
     c. Japan
     d. Papua New Guinea

14.   Which country is this?

     a. Iran
     b. Australia
     c. France
     d. Egypt

15.   Which country is this?

     a. United Kingdom
     b. South Korea
     c. Finland
     d. Norway

16. Which country is this?

    a. Chile
    b. Eritrea
    c. Montenegro
    d. Angola

17. Which country is this?

    a. Serbia
    b. Croatia
    c. Bosnia and Herzegovina
    d. Albania

18. Which country is this?

    a. Malawi
    b. Uganda
    c. Oman
    d. Azerbaijan

19. Which country is this?

    a. Argentina
    b. Bhutan
    c. Thailand
    d. Saudi Arabia

20. Which country is this?

    a. South Korea
    b. Ireland
    c. Uzbekistan
    d. Benin

North America Geography - Quiz 4

Answers on page 246

1. Jambalaya is a savoury rice dish fusing African, Spanish and French cuisines. Which US state was it developed in?

2. Which of these is NOT a city in Canada?

    a. Mississauga
    b. Syracuse
    c. Winnipeg
    d. Vancouver

3. The Dominican Republic shares the island of Hispaniola with which country?

4. Martha's Vineyard is renowned for its stunning scenery. Lying just south of Cape Cod, which US state is it in?

5. Which city has the larger population: New York City or Los Angeles?

6. Which beach in Los Angeles is famous for its boardwalk and Muscle Beach outdoor gym?

7. *Old Faithful* is a famous geyser in which US national park?

8. What's the biggest city in Texas?

9. Green Bay Packers are an NFL team based in Green Bay and have won 13 league championships, more than any other NFL side. Which state is Green Bay in?

10. In which major North American city can you go up the CN Tower, which was once the tallest free-standing tower in the world?

11. Which Canadian province is the smallest?

    a. British Columbia
    b. Prince Edward Island
    c. Saskatchewan
    d. Manitoba

12. What side of the road do people drive on in Barbados?

13. What is the approximate population of Mexico?

a. 50 million

b. 80 million

c. 130 million

d. 180 million

14. Which river does the Brooklyn Bridge, which connects Brooklyn to Manhattan, cross?

15. Which country in Central America has no Caribbean coastline?

16. What US city is known as *The City of Angels*?

17. What is the tallest building in North America?

18. What is the biggest city in Illinois?

19. San José is the capital city of which Central American country?

20. Montgomery is the capital city of which US state?

a. Kentucky

b. Mississippi

c. Alabama

d. Tennessee

South America Geography - Quiz 4

Answers on page 246

1. Which of the following countries exports the most bananas, exporting more than any country in the world?

   a. Ecuador
   b. Colombia
   c. Guyana
   d. Venezuela

2. Which country has the larger population: Peru or Chile?

3. Which city in South America has the largest carnival celebration?

4. Caracas is the capital of what country?

5. Chile is the world's largest producer of which metal?

6. Which city on Colombia's Caribbean coast has city walls that were constructed in the 16th Century to protect the city from pirates?

a. Cali

b. Bogotá

c. Cartagena

d. Buenaventura

7. Which country has the larger population: Brazil or Argentina?

8. What is the official currency of Ecuador?

   a. Ecuadorian Peso

   b. US Dollar

   c. Bitcoin

   d. Ecuadorian Real

9. What is the name of the world's largest flying bird by weight and wingspan, found along South America's Pacific Coast?

10. Brazil has the largest population of people from which Asian country outside of that country's own borders?

    a. India

    b. Japan

    c. Philippines

d. Iran

11. With how many countries does Chile share a
    land border?

12. What is the name of the active volcano near
    Quito in Ecuador that is one of the tallest in
    the world?

    a. Cotopaxi
    b. Villarrica
    c. Calbuco
    d. Cerro Toco

13. Which country in South America is the
    world's second-largest producer of farmed
    salmon?

14. What is the capital city of Brazil?

15. Which of these is NOT a city in Argentina?

    a. Córdoba
    b. Mendoza
    c. Antofagasta
    d. Buenos Aires

16. Which colourful frog is one of the most
deadly animals in the Amazon rainforest?

17. The largest lagoon in South America, Lake
Maracaibo is renowned as the place with the
most frequent lightning on Earth. Which
country is Lake Maracaibo entirely within?

18. Which of these is NOT a city in Colombia?

    a. Cusco
    b. Cali
    c. Medellín
    d. Cartagena

19. Which animal, often found in the Andes, is a
domesticated relative of the vicuña and
alpaca?

20. Which country has the larger population:
Paraguay or Uruguay?

United Kingdom Geography - Quiz 4

Answers on page 247

1. What is the national flower of Wales?

2. Chapel Down is the UK's largest wine producer. Which English county is it located in?

3. Which city in the UK has the BA postcode?

4. Crosby is a coastal town in which English county?

    a. Suffolk
    b. Northumberland
    c. Merseyside
    d. Cumbria

5. In which county in England is the New Forest primarily located?

6. Which of these is NOT a stop on the London Underground?

    a. Covent Garden
    b. Kilburn Park

c. Madewell Grove

d. White City

7. Which English city is home to the famous Clifton Suspension Bridge?

8. Which city is home to the UK's tallest building outside London?

9. Which town in England is world-famous for being the birthplace of William Shakespeare?

10. Which city is home to the UK's largest cathedral?

11. In which UK country are the Sperrin mountains located?

12. Which river runs along the border of England and Scotland?

13. Jersey, Guernsey, Alderney, and Sark are collectively known as what?

14. Which of these cities is farthest west?

a. London

b. Birmingham

c. Bristol

d. Edinburgh

15. Chapel Allerton, Headingley, and Roundhay are districts of which English city?

16. Which London Underground station is the deepest station on the network, sitting 58.5 metres below ground level?

a. Hampstead

b. Angel

c. Holborn

d. Baker Street

17. Which canal runs from Birmingham to London?

18. Which city in the UK has the EX postcode?

19. Clearwell Caves, a popular tourist attraction, is located in which forested area of Gloucestershire?

20. The Great Orme is a spectacular limestone headland located near which seaside town in North Wales?

a. Llandudno
b. Abersoch
c. Portmeirion
d. Harlech

World Geography - Quiz 5

Answers on page 248

1. What is the only country in the world that lies entirely above 1000 metres?

    a. Peru
    b. Bolivia
    c. San Marino
    d. Lesotho

2. In which country in Southeast Asia would you find the city of Dalat?

3. El Dorado International Airport serves the capital city of which South American country?

4. Where is the largest stone pyramid ever built located?

    a. Egypt
    b. Mexico
    c. Sudan
    d. USA

5. The Matterhorn is a famous peak located in which mountain range?

6. Which famous ancient trading route passed through Central Asia, connecting China with the Mediterranean?

7. What is the smallest country in the world by land area?

8. The famous wine-producing region of Rioja is located in which country?

9. What is the capital city of Ukraine?

10. Which country has the higher population: Vietnam or Thailand?

11. Which city in Turkey is famous for the Hagia Sophia and Blue Mosque?

12. Which country has the world's tallest population?

    a. Sweden
    b. Norway
    c. The Netherlands

d. South Africa

13. With an average height of 5.13ft, which
    country has the world's shortest population?

    a. Madagascar
    b. Timor Leste
    c. China
    d. Yemen

14. Which country has the longest coastline in
    the world?

15. The world's tallest arch, the Gateway Arch,
    is located in which US city?

    a. St. Louis
    b. New Orleans
    c. Chicago
    d. New York City

16. With over 3.5 million passengers travelling
    through it each day, in which country is the
    world's busiest train station?

    a. United Kingdom
    b. France

c. India

d. Japan

17. What is the official currency of the world's largest island, Greenland?

18. Tallahassee is the capital of which US state?

19. Which city in Canada is known for its French-speaking population and historic Old Port?

20. If you were skiing at the Perisher Ski Resort, which country would you be skiing in?

a. Canada

b. France

c. Australia

d. Japan

Guess the US State - Bonus Quiz

Answers on page 249

1. Which state is this?

    a. Georgia
    b. Virginia
    c. Florida
    d. New Hampshire

2. Which state is this?

    a. Kentucky
    b. California
    c. Alabama
    d. Louisiana

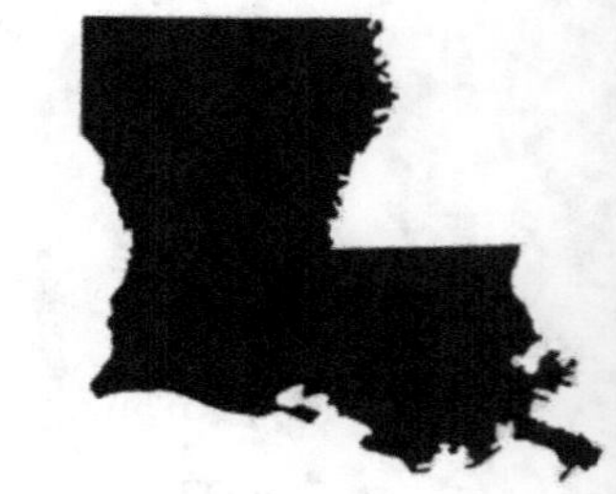

3. Which state is this?

    a. New York
    b. Texas
    c. Wyoming
    d. Utah

4. Which state is this?

    a. North Dakota
    b. South Dakota
    c. California
    d. Arizona

5. Which state is this?

    a. Pennsylvania
    b. Nevada
    c. Montana
    d. Michigan

6. Which state is this?

    a. Rhode Island
    b. Hawaii
    c. New Jersey
    d. Missouri

7. Which state is this?

    a. Alaska
    b. Illinois
    c. Nebraska
    d. Maryland

8. Which state is this?

    a. Oklahoma
    b. Oregon
    c. Kansas
    d. Arkansas

9. Which state is this?

    a. New Mexico
    b. Nevada
    c. Texas
    d. Idaho

10. Which state is this?

   a. Colorado
   b. Maine
   c. Indiana
   d. Ohio

11. Which state is this?

   a. Minnesota
   b. Wisconsin
   c. North Carolina
   d. Alaska

12. Which state is this?

   a. Oregon
   b. Utah
   c. Nevada
   d. Vermont

13. Which state is this?

a. Minnesota
b. Michigan
c. Wisconsin
d. Ohio

14. Which state is this?

a. Georgia
b. Montana
c. New Jersey
d. West Virginia

15. Which state is this?

a. Mississippi
b. Louisiana
c. Tennessee
d. Alabama

16. Which state is this?

a. Arkansas
b. Kansas
c. Idaho
d. Nebraska

17. Which state is this?

a. Wisconsin
b. Rhode Island
c. North Carolina
d. South Carolina

18. Which state is this?

a. Washington
b. Colorado
c. Nevada
d. Wyoming

19. Which state is this?

   a. Nebraska
   b. Maryland
   c. Iowa
   d. Indiana

Answers

World Geography - Quiz 1

1. Africa
2. The White House
3. Romania
4. Mediterranean Sea
5. Indonesia
6. Las Vegas
7. Iraq
8. Brazil
9. K2
10. Egypt
11. Canada
12. Saudi Riyal
13. Antarctica
14. Chile
15. New Mexico
16. One
17. Egypt
18. Monsoon
19. Ecuador
20. Japan

Africa Geography - Quiz 1

1. Somalia
2. Red
3. Algeria
4. South Africa
5. Zimbabwe
6. Indian Ocean
7. Lake Victoria
8. Namibia
9. Kenya
10. The Atlas Mountains
11. Mozambique Channel
12. Gabon
13. Malawi
14. Tanzania
15. Cape Town
16. Mediterranean Sea
17. Djibouti
18. Accra
19. English
20. The Sahara Desert

Asia Geography - Quiz 1

1. Yangtze
2. Turkmenistan

3. Lebanon

4. China and India

5. Yellow Sea

6. Hokkaido

7. Indonesia

8. India

9. Mekong River

10. Vietnam

11. Indonesia

12. Uzbekistan

13. Karachi

14. Mongolia

15. Malaysia

16. Japan

17. Vientiane

18. Gobi Desert

19. Red Sea

20. Beijing

Capital Cities - Quiz 1

1. Abu Dhabi

2. Montenegro

3. Bogota

4. Amman

5. Warsaw

6. La Paz (Bolivia)

7. Valletta (Malta)
8. Baku (Azerbaijan)
9. Honduras
10. Dublin
11. Berlin
12. Uzbekistan
13. Jakarta
14. Monrovia
15. Ethiopia
16. Asunción
17. Eritrea
18. Phnom Penh
19. Madrid
20. Ankara

Europe Geography - Quiz 1

1. Croatia
2. Hamburg
3. Bilbao
4. Portugal
5. Cannes
6. Oslo
7. France
8. Iceland
9. Batman
10. London

11. Little Mermaid

12. Genoa

13. France

14. Tenerife

15. The Cyclades

16. Albania

17. Monaco

18. Bulgaria

19. Slovenia

20. Andalucia

Geology - Quiz 1

1. Volcanic eruption

2. Igneous

3. Spain

4. The Philippines

5. 625 miles

6. Earthquakes

7. Indonesia

8. Salt Marsh

9. The Rockies

10. Australia

11. Antarctica

12. Fjords

13. Volcano

14. Firth of Forth

15. Japan
16. Northern Ireland
17. Italy
18. USA
19. South Korea
20. Fossils

Guess the Country - Quiz 1

1. Switzerland
2. Mexico
3. Portugal
4. Australia
5. New Zealand
6. Russia
7. Madagascar
8. Barbados
9. Kenya
10. Mexico
11. Indonesia
12. Jordan
13. Jamaica
14. Vietnam
15. Mozambique
16. Spain
17. New Zealand

18. Norway
19. Saudi Arabia
20. Mongolia

Landmarks - Quiz 1

1. Eiffel Tower
2. The Spanish Steps
3. The Pentagon
4. The Berlin Wall
5. Mount Rushmore
6. Verona
7. Empire State Building
8. Moscow
9. Burj Al Arab
10. Manneken Pis
11. Neuschwanstein Castle
12. Christ the Redeemer
13. Munich
14. Punjab
15. Edinburgh Castle
16. The Pantheon
17. Philadelphia
18. Kyoto
19. The Tyne Bridge
20. Malaysia

North America Geography - Quiz 1

1. Trinidad and Tobago
2. Washington
3. Nebraska
4. Minnesota
5. Bahamas
6. Turtles
7. Toronto
8. San Francisco
9. Panama Canal
10. Hoover Dam
11. Arizona
12. Yucatan
13. Kingston
14. Rhode Island
15. Blue
16. Vancouver
17. Utah
18. Chicago
19. St Lucia
20. Honduras

Oceania Geography - Quiz 1

1. Australia
2. Pacific Ocean

3. Queensland
4. True
5. Cook Strait
6. Lake Taupō
7. Marshall Islands
8. Hobart
9. Japan
10. Auckland
11. Dugongs
12. Australia
13. Australian Capital Territory
14. The Great Ocean Road
15. North Island
16. Maori
17. Sydney
18. Nauru
19. Australia
20. Sheep

Rivers, Seas & Oceans - Quiz 1

1. Pacific Ocean
2. Adriatic Sea
3. Switzerland
4. Lake Baikal
5. Mediterranean Sea
6. China (The Grand Canal)

7. Croatia
8. Madagascar
9. River Arno
10. Aegean Sea
11. River Shannon
12. Indian Ocean
13. 10
14. Gulf of Mexico
15. The Moon
16. Ghana
17. North Sea
18. Tequendama Falls
19. Glasgow
20. Pacific Ocean

South America Geography - Quiz 1

1. Chile
2. Patagonia
3. Guyana
4. Lake Titicaca
5. Christ the Redeemer
6. Panama
7. Suriname
8. Bolivia
9. Tango
10. Guyana

11. French Guiana
12. Peru
13. Ecuador
14. Oil
15. Colombia
16. Chile
17. Brazil
18. Ushuaia
19. Yellow
20. Buenos Aires

Sports Geography - Quiz 1

1. Ipswich
2. North Korea. The Rungrado 1st of May Stadium in Pyongyang.
3. Paris
4. Barcelona
5. The Netherlands
6. Sumo
7. Ice Hockey
8. Norway
9. Rugby Union
10. South Africa
11. Cricket
12. Colombia
13. Leeds

14. Melbourne
15. Football
16. Baltimore
17. Real Madrid
18. France
19. Zandvoort
20. Tokyo

United Kingdom Geography - Quiz 1

1. Rutland
2. Wiltshire
3. 18th Century (1774)
4. Southend and Stansted
5. Tamar
6. Norfolk
7. The Angel of the North
8. Anglesey
9. Leicestershire
10. Chesterfield
11. The Outer Hebrides
12. Kent
13. Loch Morar
14. Brighton
15. Coventry
16. Bath
17. Surrey

18. Carlisle

19. Penzance

20. Jurassic Coast

World Geography - Quiz 2

1. Edmonton
2. Nevada
3. Africa
4. Ireland
5. Iran
6. Tunisia
7. Eagle
8. Four
9. Pacific Ocean
10. China
11. Australia
12. Africa
13. Saudi Arabia
14. Abuja
15. Dubai
16. Suriname
17. São Paulo
18. The Antarctic
19. Maldives
20. New Zealand

Africa Geography - Quiz 2

1. Senegal
2. Egypt
3. Kalahari Desert
4. South Africa
5. Malawi
6. Nigeria
7. Portuguese
8. Tanzania
9. Algiers
10. Angola
11. Indian Ocean
12. Johannesburg
13. French
14. Egypt
15. Vanilla
16. The Serengeti
17. Lagos
18. Burundi
19. Ethiopia
20. Egypt

Asia Geography - Quiz 2

1. China
2. Persian Gulf

3. Saudi Arabia
4. Cambodia
5. Pakistan
6. Kuala Lumpur
7. Thailand
8. Singapore
9. Petra
10. Nepal
11. India
12. Philippines
13. China
14. Borneo
15. Lion
16. Uttarakhand
17. Yokohama
18. Taiwan
19. The Black Sea
20. South Korea (Incheon International Airport is in Seoul)

Capital Cities - Quiz 2

1. Muscat
2. Colombo
3. Ulaanbaatar
4. Canberra
5. Burkina Faso

6. Amsterdam
7. The Seychelles
8. Zagreb
9. Argentina
10. Moscow
11. Skopje
12. Lisbon
13. Bridgetown
14. Baghdad
15. Manama
16. Pyongyang
17. Apia
18. New Delhi
19. Beijing
20. Stockholm

Europe Geography - Quiz 2

1. Rome
2. Bulgaria
3. Barcelona
4. Finland
5. Portugal
6. Italy
7. Copenhagen
8. Corsica
9. Piccadilly Circus

10. The Hague
11. Slovenia
12. Czech Republic
13. Leeds
14. Lecce
15. Vienna
16. Lisbon
17. Romania
18. Black Forest
19. Bulgaria
20. Paris (The Louvre)

Geology - Quiz 2

1. Ethiopia
2. Chihuahua
3. Indonesia
4. El Popo
5. Lava
6. Dallol
7. Sandstone
8. Metamorphic
9. Pangaea
10. Mantle
11. The Pacific Plate
12. Glacier
13. Diamond

14. Erosion
15. Mountain range
16. Iron
17. Blue
18. Krakatoa
19. Chalk
20. Caves

Guess the Country - Quiz 2

1. South Africa
2. Cuba
3. Sri Lanka
4. Portugal
5. Philippines
6. Cyprus
7. The Netherlands
8. Yemen
9. United Kingdom (Brooklands in Surrey)
10. Iceland
11. Bulgaria
12. Sweden
13. Greece
14. The Philippines
15. Nigeria
16. Poland
17. Portugal

18. Trinidad and Tobago
19. Bolivia (37 official languages)
20. Ireland

Landmarks - Quiz 2

1. The Alhambra
2. The Shard
3. Hollywood Boulevard
4. Antoni Gaudí
5. Iceland
6. Japan
7. Madrid
8. The Great Sphinx of Giza
9. Trafalgar Square
10. Ellis Island
11. Seville
12. New Orleans
13. Ponte Vecchio
14. Argentina
15. Athens
16. Porto
17. Tate Modern
18. Las Vegas
19. Vietnam
20. France

North America Geography - Quiz 2

1. Sacramento
2. Montana
3. Alberta
4. Cuba
5. Florida
6. South Dakota
7. Alaska
8. Georgia
9. Toronto
10. Michigan
11. True, in 1968
12. San Francisco Bay
13. Niagara Falls
14. British Columbia
15. Arizona
16. Chihuahua
17. Chicago
18. Death Valley
19. Hawaii
20. Mississippi River

Oceania Geography - Quiz 2

1. Australia
2. South Australia

3. Christchurch
4. Funafuti
5. Southern Alps
6. Tasmania
7. New Guinea Rainforest
8. Napier
9. Queensland
10. Bismarck Archipelago
11. 10
12. Murray River
13. 5 million
14. The Outback
15. Tropical climate
16. Vanuatu
17. 25 million
18. Australia
19. Port Moresby
20. Christmas Island

Rivers, Seas & Oceans - Quiz 2

1. Lake Windermere
2. South America
3. Arctic Ocean
4. Lake Chapala
5. Angel Falls
6. Palk Strait

7. Texas
8. Magdalena
9. Suez Canal
10. Zambezi River
11. Botswana
12. Dominican Republic
13. Tagus
14. The Euphrates River
15. The River Douro
16. Tasman Sea
17. The Congo River
18. The Danube River
19. The Yangtze River
20. Angola

South America Geography - Quiz 2

1. Dead Woman's Pass
2. Bogota
3. Chile
4. Uruguay
5. Brazil (Rio de Janeiro in 2016)
6. Montevideo
7. Peru
8. Paraguay
9. Argentina
10. Jaguar

11. Soybeans
12. Spectacled Bear
13. Rio de Janeiro
14. Bolivia
15. Rainbow Mountain
16. Colombian peso
17. The Andes
18. Peru
19. 20 million
20. Argentina

Sports Geography - Quiz 2

1. New Zealand
2. USA
3. Cristiano Ronaldo
4. Newlands
5. New Jersey
6. Sumo
7. South Africa
8. Salt Lake City
9. Argentina
10. Baseball
11. Camp Nou
12. New York City
13. Peru
14. The Australian Open

15. Monaco

16. Madagascar

17. France

18. Los Angeles

19. Golf

20. American Football

United Kingdom Geography - Quiz 2

1. Islay

2. Truro

3. Lake District

4. M6

5. Liverpool

6. Ben Nevis

7. Shetland

8. Regent's Park

9. Kent

10. Cornwall

11. Southend-on-Sea (1.33 miles)

12. Cairngorms National Park

13. York

14. River Tay

15. Norwich

16. Staffordshire

17. Aberdeen

18. The Bullring

19. Whitley Bay

20. Bristol

World Geography - Quiz 3

1. Bay of Bengal
2. Flat-Top Mountain
3. The Congo
4. French
5. Africa
6. Namib Desert
7. Argentina
8. Canada
9. The Bosporus Strait
10. Arctic Ocean
11. Chile
12. The Nile
13. Brazil (locally known as Praia do Cassino)
14. Bucharest, Romania
15. Mexico
16. Death Valley. Furnace Creek in Death Valley, where a temperature of 56.7°C was recorded on 10th July 1913
17. Munich
18. Pan-American Highway (19,000 miles)

19. Sweden. Sweden has the most islands in the world, with 267,570. The majority of these islands are uninhabited.
20. Hells Canyon

Africa Geography - Quiz 3

1. Baobab
2. Algeria
3. Naira
4. Benin
5. Botswana
6. Cape Town
7. Portuguese
8. Ivory Coast (Côte d'Ivoire)
9. Lake Malawi
10. Uganda
11. Mali
12. Nigeria (230 million)
13. Khartoum
14. Togo
15. The Democratic Republic of the Congo (DRC)
16. Angola
17. Kruger National Park
18. Morocco
19. The Gambia

20. Johannesburg

Asia Geography - Quiz 3

1. Sri Lanka
2. Kazakhstan and Turkmenistan
3. Indian Rupee (INR)
4. Japan
5. Islamabad
6. Shanghai
7. Bengali
8. Sri Lanka
9. Israel and Jordan
10. Hiroshima
11. The Himalayas
12. The Caspian Sea
13. Laos
14. Jaipur
15. Taipei
16. 100 million
17. Cherry Blossom (Sakura)
18. Chao Phraya River
19. Chennai
20. The Philippines

Capital Cities - Quiz 3

1. Athens
2. Valletta
3. Nouakchott
4. Baku
5. Bern
6. Tokyo
7. Minsk
8. Ashgabat
9. Beijing
10. Tbilisi
11. Washington DC
12. Tehran
13. Ngerulmud, Palau
14. Kazakhstan
15. Latvia
16. Rome
17. Bamako
18. Gaborone
19. Wellington, New Zealand
20. Budapest

Europe Geography - Quiz 3

1. Florence
2. Spain

3. Crete
4. Sardinia
5. Croatia
6. Hungary
7. Seville
8. Portugal
9. Turkey
10. Budapest (Dohány Street Synagogue)
11. Bordeaux
12. Estonia, Latvia, Lithuania
13. The Carpathian Mountains
14. Lake Geneva
15. Mallorca
16. Amsterdam
17. Venice
18. Prague
19. Lake Garda
20. Windsor Castle

Guess the Country - Quiz 3

1. Peru
2. Germany
3. USA
4. Somalia
5. Brazil
6. Sri Lanka

7. Portugal
8. The Gambia
9. Jamaica
10. Vietnam
11. New Zealand
12. Egypt
13. United Arab Emirates
14. The Netherlands
15. Norway
16. Austria
17. Iceland
18. Namibia
19. Japan
20. Chile

North America Geography - Quiz 3

1. Hollywood Sign
2. Boston
3. Miami
4. California
5. Newfoundland and Labrador
6. Georgia
7. Pacific
8. Hawaii
9. Yellowstone
10. Nashville

11. Utah
12. Jamaica
13. Seattle
14. 3 times
15. West Virginia
16. 2005
17. California
18. Great Salt Lake
19. Missouri
20. Halifax

Oceania Geography - Quiz 3

1. Rugby Union
2. The Great Dividing Range
3. Sydney
4. Dunedin Airport
5. Perth
6. Shiraz
7. White Island
8. Uluru / Ayers Rock
9. Shark Bay
10. Blue Mountains
11. True
12. Brisbane
13. North Island
14. Nukuʻalofa

15. Queensland

16. Fiji

17. Rugby League

18. Melbourne

19. Kangaroo

20. Brisbane

Rivers, Seas & Oceans - Quiz 3

1. Paraná River

2. Pacific Ocean

3. Arctic Ocean

4. Atoll

5. Atlantic Ocean

6. River Trent

7. Puerto Rico Trench

8. The Philippines

9. Suez Canal

10. Atlantic Ocean

11. River Morar

12. Indian Ocean

13. Russia

14. North Sea

15. River Danube

16. Five

17. Chicago River

18. Switzerland (Rhein Falls)

19. Amstel River
20. Pacific Ocean

South America Geography - Quiz 3

1. Argentina
2. Medellin
3. Paraguay
4. Uruguay
5. Panama
6. Chile
7. Brazil
8. Argentina
9. Venezuela
10. Ecuador
11. Colombia
12. Argentina
13. Bolivia
14. Chile
15. Potatoes
16. Argentina
17. Suriname
18. 34 million
19. Brazil
20. Colombia

Sports Geography - Quiz 3

1. Baseball
2. Alexandra Palace
3. Switzerland
4. London with 22 stadiums
5. Germany
6. Football
7. Bath Rugby
8. Golf
9. Inter Milan
10. Baseball
11. Ireland
12. Table Tennis
13. Mexico
14. Napoli
15. Toronto
16. Sailing
17. Australia
18. Oil Wrestling
19. Sunderland
20. Brazil

United Kingdom Geography - Quiz 3

1. Leicestershire
2. Tower Hamlets

3. Nottinghamshire
4. Ben Macdui
5. East Sussex
6. Isle of Man
7. Manchester
8. Whisky
9. North York Moors National Park
10. Northern Line
11. Berkshire
12. Northern Ireland
13. Inverness
14. The Pennines
15. M6
16. Belfast
17. The Solent
18. The River Mersey
19. North Yorkshire
20. The Royal Mile

World Geography - Quiz 4

1. The Trans-Siberian Railway
2. Edinburgh of the Seven Seas
3. Mexico
4. China
5. South Korea
6. Northern Territory

7. Asian
8. Caribbean Sea
9. Arizona
10. Sea of Marmara
11. Reykjavik, Iceland
12. Atlantic Ocean
13. USA
14. Colombia
15. Canada
16. New Delhi
17. Chile
18. New York City
19. Hawaii
20. Australia

Africa Geography - Quiz 4

1. Oran
2. Nairobi
3. Sudan
4. Copper
5. Springbok
6. Zimbabwe
7. False. The giraffe is Tanzania's national animal
8. Mauritius
9. Egypt

10. Windhoek
11. Swahili
12. Réunion
13. Prison
14. Ivory Coast
15. Flamingo - millions congregate here
16. Democratic Republic of the Congo
17. Somali Shilling
18. Ethiopia
19. Zambezi River
20. Tanzania

Asia Geography - Quiz 4

1. Sri Lanka
2. Left-hand side
3. Train
4. Vietnam
5. Taj Mahal
6. Football
7. Rupiah
8. Bhutan
9. Giant Panda
10. Pakistan
11. Yangon
12. Kathmandu
13. Green

14. Mount Fuji
15. Myanmar
16. Mango
17. Shanghai
18. Nepal
19. Vietnam
20. Mumbai

Europe Geography - Quiz 4

1. Crete
2. Braga
3. Denmark
4. Wolfsburg
5. Ural Mountains
6. Sicily
7. Barcelona
8. Sweden
9. Germany
10. Rome
11. Turkey
12. St Petersburg
13. Hamburg
14. Tirana
15. Copenhagen
16. Germany
17. St. Mark's Square (Piazza San Marco)

18. Rotterdam
19. Dunkirk
20. Italy

Guess the Country - Quiz 4

1. France
2. Mexico
3. India
4. Denmark
5. Australia
6. Cuba
7. Italy
8. Cyprus
9. Algeria
10. Madagascar
11. Argentina
12. Estonia
13. North Korea
14. Iran
15. Finland
16. Eritrea
17. Croatia
18. Malawi
19. Thailand
20. Benin

North America Geography - Quiz 4

1. Louisiana
2. Syracuse
3. Haiti
4. Massachusetts
5. New York City
6. Venice Beach
7. Yellowstone
8. Houston
9. Wisconsin
10. Toronto
11. Prince Edward Island
12. Left-hand side
13. 130 million
14. East River
15. El Salvador
16. Los Angeles
17. One World Trade Center
18. Chicago
19. Costa Rica
20. Alabama

South America Geography - Quiz 4

1. Ecuador
2. Peru

3. Rio de Janeiro

4. Venezuela

5. Copper

6. Cartagena

7. Brazil

8. US Dollar

9. Andean Condor

10. Japan

11. Three

12. Cotopaxi

13. Chile

14. Brasilia

15. Antofagasta

16. Poison Dart Frog

17. Venezuela

18. Maracaibo

19. Llama

20. Paraguay

United Kingdom Geography - Quiz 4

1. Daffodil

2. Kent

3. Bath

4. Merseyside

5. Hampshire

6. Madewell Grove

7. Bristol
8. Manchester
9. Stratford-upon-Avon
10. Liverpool
11. Northern Ireland
12. River Tweed
13. The Channel Islands
14. Edinburgh
15. Leeds
16. Hampstead
17. The Grand Union Canal
18. Exeter
19. Forest of Dean
20. Llandudno

World Geography - Quiz 5

1. Lesotho
2. Vietnam
3. Colombia
4. Mexico
5. The Alps
6. The Silk Road
7. Vatican City
8. Spain
9. Kyiv
10. Vietnam

11. Istanbul

12. The Netherlands

13. Timor Leste (East Timor)

14. Canada

15. St. Louis

16. Japan

17. Danish Krone

18. Florida

19. Montreal

20. Australia

Guess the US State - Bonus

1. Florida

2. Louisiana

3. New York

4. California

5. Nevada

6. Hawaii

7. Illinois

8. Oklahoma

9. Texas

10. Colorado

11. Alaska

12. Oregon

13. Michigan

14. Montana

15. Tennessee
16. Arkansas
17. Rhode Island
18. Washington
19. Iowa

www.ingramcontent.com/pod-product-compliance
Lightning Source LLC
Chambersburg PA
CBHW051553250726
48653CB00004BA/1125